Look—and Learn!

Other Beeline Books Include:

The Publishing Center
How to Create a Successful Publishing Center in Your School, Church, or Community Group

The Treasured Mailbox
How to Use Authentic Correspondence with Children, K–6

Inside the Classroom
Teaching Kindergarten and First Grade

Write-A-Thon
How to Conduct a Writing Marathon in Your Third-to-Fifth Grade Class

The Magical Classroom
Exploring Science, Language, and Perception with Children

Walk This Way!
Classroom Hikes to Learning

Kids on the 'Net
Conducting Internet Research in K–5 Classrooms

The Young Author Festival Handbook
What Every Planner Needs to Know

Look—and Learn!

Using Picture Books in Grades Five Through Eight

Sheryl Lee Saunders 8 August 2001

bee line BOOKS

Heinemann
Portsmouth, NH

To David and Tully

Heinemann
A division of Reed Elsevier Inc.
361 Hanover Street
Portsmouth, NH 03801–3912
http://www.heinemann.com

Offices and agents throughout the world

The author and publisher wish to thank those who have generously given permission to reprint borrowed material:

"December" from *January Rides the Wind: A Book of Months* by Charlotte E. Otten. Text copyright © 1997 by Charlotte E. Otten. By permission of Lothrop, Lee & Shepard Books, an imprint of Morrow Junior Books, a division of William Morrow and Company, Inc.

Library of Congress Cataloging-in-Publication Data
Saunders, Sheryl Lee.
Look—and learn! : using picture books in grades five through eight / Sheryl Lee Saunders.
p. cm.
Includes bibliographical references.
ISBN 0-325-00019-0 (alk. paper)
1. Picture books for children—Educational aspects. 2. School children—Books and reading. 3. Education, Elementary—Activity programs. I. Title.
LB1044.9.P49S29 1999
372.13'2—dc21 98-31489
CIP

Editor: Amy Cohn
Production: Elizabeth Valway
Interior design: Greta D. Sibley & Associates
Cover design: Darci Mehall/Aureo Design
Manufacturing: Louise Richardson

Printed in the United States of America on acid-free paper
03 02 01 00 99 ML 2 3 4 5

Contents

Introduction

The Case for Picture Books with Older Readers

> The picture book is a peculiar art form that thrives on genius, intuition, daring and a meticulous attention to its history and its various, complex components. The picture book is a picture puzzle, badly misunderstood by critics and condescended to by far too many as merely a trifle for "the kiddies."
>
> —Maurice Sendak, Foreword to *George and Martha: The Complete Stories of Two Best Friends*

My career in elementary education began in 1979, teaching first graders at a public school in the Rocky Mountains of Colorado. I found myself using picture books—much to my students' delight and benefit—to teach reading, math, social studies, and science. I deemed the picture book to be one of the most effective educational tools that I employed on a daily basis, and I also discovered that my affinity for this genre of children's literature was both profound and permanent.

Then, in 1995, after an eight-year hiatus during which I earned a master's degree in children's literature and began raising a child, I returned to teaching. My students were a multiaged group of seven- through twelve-year-olds at a tiny Montessori school in a small, quaint New Hampshire town. Again, I turned to that entity that has since become as familiar as pencils, paper, tables, and chairs in elementary classrooms throughout the country: the picture book.

My experience there confirmed for me the belief that the picture book is remarkably well suited for children not only in a multiaged classroom, but also in the intermediate grades. Picture books may enrich and instruct even seventh and eighth graders as well. There are a handful of compelling reasons that argue for the presence of picture books in older readers' classrooms; a few of them follow.

First, picture books are finite in length, short enough to be read in one sitting. With precious little classroom instructional time, teachers and their students can read a picture book from start to finish and still have time for meaningful subsequent assignments, discussions, or activities.

Second, picture books often contain intriguing illustrations and are pleasurable to view. Visual and graphic, picture books provide an astonishingly rich array of art styles and media and offer endless aesthetic learning opportunities for older readers. This notion was recognized over three hundred years ago by a Moravian bishop named Johann Amos Comenius (1592–1670), who, just like you, was a teacher.

In 1658, he created what is recognized as the first picture book ever made expressly for children. Entitled *Orbis Sensualium Pictus (The Visible World in Pictures)* but most often referred to as *Orbis Pictus*, Comenius' creation was a Latin text book with a series of woodcuts that depicted everyday objects, a picture dictionary of sorts.

Comenius was a visionary educator who wanted children to learn about and enjoy Nature's creations rather than simply memorize abstract knowledge. And he was among the first to appreciate the belief that children will remember things best if they see them. My classroom experience convinces me that Comenius was indeed sagacious in his observations. I contend that today's students who read picture books—with their words *and* pictures—not only increase their understanding of the world, but also have fun doing so.

Third, picture book texts, with their trademark brevity, contain carefully considered and chosen words, sometimes poetic and almost always narrative in their nature. The texts often serve as noteworthy writing models for students' original writings. From picture books, students may gain a rich conciseness of language, a tremendous sense of story, and a diversity of voices, all of which augment their developing writing skills.

Fourth, picture books are reader-friendly; students may "relax" when reading them. With picture books, those young people are allowed to let down their inhibitions regarding reading, something that rarely happens when learning transpires in the content areas, especially when esoteric, arcane textbooks are used. I maintain that students who are exposed to excellent, reader-friendly picture books are far more likely to become lifelong readers than are those who read only classroom textbooks.

Finally, picture books, with their seamless partnership of pictures and words, can easily integrate many aspects of curricula, allowing older readers to make important connections among different subjects, providing them a grasp of what I have always labeled "the big picture." An understanding of that big picture further affords them opportunities to develop the habit of connecting picture books to their own life experiences, which I believe ultimately enhances these students' chances of becoming lifelong learners and lifelong readers.

Older students bring sophistication, experience, and a great deal of reader history to a picture book. One needs only to look to David Macaulay's *Shortcut* (Houghton, 1995) or Chris Van Allsburg's *The Wreck of the Zephyr* (Houghton, 1983) to recognize the power of such picture books to reach a wider, more receptive audience. My mission in writing this book is to convey to teachers some of the vast potential I believe the picture book holds for use in their own classrooms; the educational rewards of sharing picture books with older readers, for student and teacher alike, are without limit.

Author's Note

This book is designed to permit its use without having to read it from beginning to end. I have arranged the chapters by themes, selecting topics widely covered in the intermediate grades, especially by those teachers who implement theme studies in their classrooms. In nearly all chapters, I have attempted to write about the newest and noteworthiest picture books available today, in part, because I know firsthand how challenging and time-consuming it is to keep current in the field of children's literature. With more than five thousand books published annually in the United States alone, that task can be daunting and enormous.

I cannot stress enough how important it is to read this book in conjunction with one or two of the picture books discussed in detail. It is not essential to do so, but it is much more meaningful. Enlist the aid of your school librarians; ask if they have any of these titles on hand. If not, ask if they might order two or three—and sit down together with those books—and this one!—when they arrive.

I categorize each picture book title first by genre, then share a brief plot synopsis and critical commentary. When evaluating illustrations, I examine the customary visual elements of design of line, shape, color, value, and texture. Remarks regarding the texts often include a discussion of such literary elements as character, plot, setting, theme, style, and so on. Finally,

I may highlight notable attributes found only in picture books: the interplay between words and pictures, the drama of the turning of each page, or design and format.

When working with picture books and older students, I discuss these very same elements and attributes, articulating my thoughts in a similar fashion. Given such exposure and opportunity, the students themselves become capable picture book critics; I encourage you to do so with your own class.

You may find it ironic that in this book about picture books there aren't any pictures. That's deliberate. It's too easy merely to glance at a picture provided and not see what it reveals. With my words, I want you to see the images in your mind's eye. With my words, I want you to develop the acumen to judge for yourself the potential of any individual title you might come across, not just the books described here.

Several suggested teaching activities follow, activities in which you and your students may engage. The ideas I offer reinforce the notion that students interacting with "real books" should be ensconced in learning experiences that nurture and develop an integration of their reading, speaking, writing, and listening skills. Reading real books enhances creative expression within all aspects of the curricula: social studies, science, art, music, mathematics, and language arts.

For variety's sake, I offer individual, small-group, and plenary-group activities. By no means are my suggestions meant to be exhaustive; I hope that the ideas might serve as fodder for an even richer classroom experience that you customize specifically for your students. Please remember: You know best your students' learning dispositions, and you can best tailor a literature response that suits them ideally.

The picture books I selected are all in print today, with some of them available in less costly paperback versions. Title availability and affordability certainly figure into a teacher's decision to purchase a particular book, whether buying multiple copies for literature groups or simply one copy for a classroom library collection.

Please note that each *For Further Reading* section lists books that are widely available and often considered classic. There are only a handful of titles that are older; I include them when I believe that they are so significant they deserve being discussed, even among newer books. But I don't ignore these long-beloved chestnuts, either.

When I have seen such lists for further reading at the backs of many books, I usually skip over them because I am not always sure what they're supposed to mean. I'm not sure which titles I want to search for and consider, which I don't. There's simply not enough information. So, I've included a short annotation that I hope informs you. Subject matter, plot description, and a brief critical remark should help you decide where in your curriculum you might use a particular book. I hope you find the titles on the supplemental lists just as exciting—and important—as the ones described in greater detail. I am sure you and your students will delight in them just as much.

As you read, please keep in mind the following thought from that visionary educator, Comenius, who stated over three centuries ago: "For it is apparent that Children (even from their Infancy almost) are delighted with Pictures, and willingly please their eyes with these sights." Like Comenius, I contend that if you use these picture books and others like them with older children, the results will satisfy teachers and students alike.

Chapter 1

War and Conflict

Historical Fiction

> A picturebook is text, illustrations, total design; an item of manufacture and a commercial product; a social, cultural, historical document . . .
>
> —Barbara Bader, *American Picturebooks from Noah's Ark to the Beast Within*

For contemporary children, the concept of war remains so far removed from their daily lives it seems nearly impossible for them to comprehend. Some might vaguely recall America's Desert Storm Operation; others might have an inkling of what's happening in Bosnia or be aware of the present strife in the Middle East. For the most part, however, war to today's youngsters is history, just a thing of the past. And what our children do know about armed conflict is often a scanty handful of facts that include dates, names of generals, or important battles. Some children are even hard put to chronicle the wars the United States has participated in, not fully knowing when and why these battles were even waged.

Picture books offer intermediate-grade students far more than names, dates, and places. With their felicitous combinations of text and illustrations, picture books about war offer graphic images that corroborate powerful words, and they do so in a comprehendable yet memorable fashion. Picture books about war take an intangible, complex issue and make it more approachable and hence, easier to understand.

Ultimately, these kinds of picture books allow most students to think of the genre of historical fiction as far more than a means of conveying factual information about the past within an imagined context. The words in picture books give students stories to ponder, poignant stories about people, oftentimes just like themselves; the illustrations in picture books provide a sense of place and give face to characters with whom children today may identify.

Some picture books about war may serve as inviting introductions to the particular historical era you want to study, while others may concentrate on a specific event that transpired on a certain date. I believe that whatever their focus, these picture books contain the power to enliven, educate, and engage students in history in hopes of gaining a better understanding of their world today.

The following picture book titles discuss the United States' devastating Civil War, from two Union soldiers' perspectives as well as that of one President; World War II and an intrepid rescue, as well as its heinous Holocaust; the much-maligned Vietnam War and its lasting impact.

As a classroom teacher, I discovered that the power these books possessed fostered effortless sharing. The students grasped these historical times in ways I had rarely observed when they read only textbooks about the same subject matter. The students connected to these telling incidents; battles, dates, and names of leaders and generals came alive. These are not books for kindergartners; these are picture books for mature children, able to tackle mature themes.

Pink and Say

Patricia Polacco. 1994. *Pink and Say.* New York: Philomel.
ISBN 0-399-22671-0

Synopsis

Patricia Polacco's *Pink and Say* is fictionalized family history. The family story the author–illustrator so poignantly shares tells about the fortuitous meeting during the Civil War of two young Union soldiers—one of whom was Polacco's own great-great-grandfather.

Sheldon Curtis, or "Say," is fifteen years old when he is seriously wounded and left for dead on a Georgia battlefield. Pinkus Aylee, or "Pink," born a slave, is also a young Union soldier. He finds Say and brings him to the home of his mother, who lives nearby. Pink's mother, Moe Moe Bay, nurses Say back to health.

Pink and Say are Union soldiers in Confederate territory where marauding southern troops are on the rampage. They realize the extent of the danger they face, so they hide. Moe Moe Bay protects them, and pays with her life.

The two then head north to return to their respective Union outfits but are soon captured by Confederate soldiers. Pink and Say both become prisoners at the notorious Andersonville prison. Shortly thereafter, Pink is hanged. Say scarcely survives his incarceration and eventually returns home to his family.

Polacco's signature artwork, folksy watercolor and pencil illustrations, captures the pain and suffering of the War Between the States as experienced by these two young men from different races. Note especially the only two-page spread with no text: Transporting the near-dead Say, Pink looks out from a shallow rocky ditch, his eyes carefully searching for signs of the enemy ahead. One mahogany-brown hand grasps a clump of forest grass for support; his other arm wraps around Say's chest. The two uniformed young men seem almost fixed in that trench. Their monumentality emphasizes the sculpture-like, *Pietà*-like poses Polacco gives Pink and Say throughout the powerful story, and helps to etch forever in readers' memories their plight and the calamity of the Civil War.

Using a subdued, somber palette of dreary blues, sanguinary reds, and muddy browns, Polacco masterfully conveys the atrocious nature of the worst war in U.S. history. Her portrayals of Pink and Say also exemplify the steadfast friendship they enjoy, and celebrate the humanity these two exhibit in the midst of such inhumanity.

Suggested Activities

- Conduct an in-depth study of Andersonville, one of the Confederates' prisoner of war camps. At the war's end more than thirty thousand Union soldiers were held captive there; over ten thousand of them succumbed to starvation and disease. Keeping in mind the ghastly conditions of such prisons, create five journal entries that Say Curtis might have written while incarcerated there; share with the entire class.
- With a group of classmates, learn the words and melody of "John Brown's Body," a popular marching song sung by nearly everyone in the North; research the real John Brown. He existed, and this song was written for him. Or investigate the importance of singing in the Civil War and learn other songs still well known today, such as "Dixie Land," "When Johnny Comes Marching Home," and "Goober Peas."
- During a themed unit of study of the Civil War, read aloud Irene Hunt's *Across Five Aprils* (1964), one of the most critically acclaimed historical novels published in American children's literature. Naive Illinois farmboy Jethro Creighton, age nine in April 1861, grows quickly to manhood during the tragic years of the Civil War. (Research also suggests that students are more apt to choose a book to read on their own if they have heard it first as a read-aloud.)
- Invite students to ask their grandparents or great aunts and uncles if there is a poignant tale within their own family history; be prepared to tell how many generations old their family tale is, and who passed it on to whom, and so on; share that story orally with the class. Be certain to instruct the students that, in telling their stories, they should pay particular attention to body language, voice inflection, and how they might alter the pace of their tale to emphasize drama.
- In the illustrations, Patricia Polacco cleverly incorporates reproductions of her own relatives' photographs to express a familial involvement in her story; create a photomontage of your own family tree, going back as many generations as you possibly can; make a classroom display.

The Gettysburg Address

Abraham Lincoln. 1995. *The Gettysburg Address.* Illustrated by Michael McCurdy. Boston: Houghton Mifflin. ISBN 0-395-69824-3

Synopsis

The entire text of this stellar picture book—only 272 words—was spoken on November 19, 1863, by perhaps one of the greatest presidents the United States has ever known. Some historians proclaim Lincoln's three-minute talk that day one of the greatest speeches ever written. Lincoln's intention was to honor the Yankee soldiers who died at the Battle of Gettysburg and to explain to citizens the meaning of the Civil War. Lincoln and his critics would never imagine that he succeeded in doing far more. His words reverberate today with the same truth they did in 1863 because they describe so succinctly the foundations of U.S. values and our nation's philosophy. About "The Gettysburg Address," historian Gary Wills aptly writes in the book's foreword: "It is the best example in history of the fact that nothing is more practical than idealism, that ideas matter, that words are more important than weapons."

Artist Michael McCurdy's evocative, detailed black-and-white scratchboard illustrations also resonate throughout the thirty-two pages of the strikingly designed picture book. Like Lincoln's memorable speech, the illustrations are vivid, powerful, and unforgettable. Using a medium that is reminiscent of the era itself, McCurdy delivers artwork that spectacularly amplifies the drama and the intensity Lincoln's words connote.

Opposite the title page appears Lincoln: Tall and slender in a slightly rumpled suit and bowtie askew, he grasps his prepared speech in his right hand. This president stands against and in the middle of a background split vertically with contrasting black and white, which suggests a nation divided. Minute, fine lines mark Lincoln's face; his is a sad, tired, but resolute countenance.

Throughout the book, McCurdy's portraits of President Lincoln stand larger than life, convincing readers that this statesman is powerful enough to win alone a contest as searing as a civil war. Sweeping double-page spreads depict slaves, Union and Confederate soldiers, and civilians, all of whom are embroiled in the strife; this picture book is ideal for plenary-group sharing.

Suggested Activities

• Obtain a copy of Dr. Martin Luther King, Jr.'s "I Have A Dream" speech. Using a Venn diagram, compare and contrast the two speeches for language, style, and content. Imagine rewriting each of these speeches for the 1990s; what language would you keep, what words would you change to savor anew the messages contained within each?

• Have the students imagine themselves as newspaper reporters from either the North or the South. Depending on their Northern or Southern viewpoint, they will write articles for a newspaper that critiques Lincoln's "Gettysburg Address."

• Investigate the assassination of President Abraham Lincoln to uncover some of the many mysteries that still surround his murder. Focus on the questions regarding whether the Confederates conspired to kill Lincoln; look closely at Lincoln's own premonitions that foreshadowed his death.

• Compile as many poems as you can about President Lincoln's life or assassination; be certain to include Walt Whitman's "Oh Captain, My Captain!," Eve Merriam's "To Meet Mr. Lincoln," and an untitled tribute to Lincoln written by Herman Melville. Create a Lincoln anthology that includes student-drawn illustrations. Have some students commit the poems to memory, and present a recitation program for classroom parents or another class.

• Hold a classroom debate modeled after the great Lincoln–Douglas debates that took place in 1858, when both men were campaigning for the U.S. Senate. Be prepared to share your facts and opinions about slavery from a moral, political, and legal point of view.

• Write to Gettysburg National Park in Gettysburg, Pennsylvania. After perusing the printed matter you receive, create your own travel brochure for prospective tourists. Provide your own artwork and write your own text after carefully considering what you would want visitors to experience at the historic site.

The Little Ships: The Heroic Rescue at Dunkirk in World War II

Louise Borden. 1997. *The Little Ships: The Heroic Rescue at Dunkirk in World War II.* Illustrated by Michael Foreman. New York: McElderry Books. ISBN 0-689-80827-5

Synopsis

Author Louise Borden provides a superb fictional account of the actual rescue in 1940 of over 300,000 British and French soldiers trapped at Dunkirk in France by Nazi Germany troops. More than eight hundred civilian vessels—small fishing boats, tugboats, and coastal river craft—helped the larger British Royal Navy ships safely ferry the stranded Allied troops across the forty-five-mile distance of the English Channel to Great Britain's Dover and nearby ports.

In a vivid first-person voice, a young English girl tells how she and her fisherman father, aboard their own small boat, the *Lucy*, participated in that daring and dangerous rescue adventure. Through a convincing heroine's eyes and ears—"she could set an anchor and coil a rope and nudge speed into the *Lucy's* old engine better than some of the village men"—readers experience the sights and sounds of wartime havoc, as thousands of beleaguered men, hundreds of riderless horses, and dozens of stray dogs boarded the "little ships" in shallow water and were then transported to big naval ships anchored in deeper waters.

Michael Foreman's consummate watercolor illustrations portray the impressive flotilla in appropriately drab hues of "uniform brown and battleship gray" as the nearly five-mile-long convoy passes silently through the cerulean blue waters. The narrative content of Foreman's pictures tells much: In the young girl's face and the numerous countenances of the soldiers, readers witness the devastating toll that World War II exacted on everyone involved.

Suggested Activities

• At book's end, the young girl keeps a little black dog that a French sergeant had given her and names him Smoky Joe; create a watercolor painting of Smoky Joe, and write an acrostic poem using the dog's name (SMOKY JOE), all about the little ships' rescue operation from the dog's point of view.

- To help pinpoint the setting, have a small group of students create a mural-sized map of the English Channel and the French and British coasts; plot the route of the armada of the little ships; include a map legend and compass rose, and make it colorful. Have the group present it to the entire class.
- The little ships' rescue operation lasted nine days, from May 26 through June 4, 1940; imagine you are an owner of one of the small boats and write nine journal entries that would tell of your courageous experience.
- Write to the British Royal Navy, asking for more written materials about this heroic occasion; if possible, draft a class letter—an interview of sorts—to a person who was involved in this event, asking them to write back.
- The little ships saved the Allied troops at Dunkirk, but they couldn't save France. On June 14, 1940, German tanks rolled into Paris, and Hitler then occupied France. On a narrow roll of paper, make a classroom time line of the events that followed after that occupation, recounting the things that happened in France until Germany surrendered; display this in the classroom.
- Research the life and accomplishments of Winston Churchill, Britain's famous leader during World War II. Prepare a skit in which Churchill shares teatime with the young girl, her fisherman father, and her brother, John, a British soldier—all characters from the picture book. Strive for authentic dialogue and English accents; present it to another class studying World War II.

Star of Fear, Star of Hope

Jo Hoestlandt. 1995. *Star of Fear, Star of Hope.* Illustrated by Johanna Kang. Translated from French by Mark Polizzotti. New York: Walker and Company. ISBN 0-8027-8373-2

Synopsis

The text of this compelling picture book begins this way: "My name is Helen, and I'm nearly an old woman now. When I'm gone, who will remember Lydia? That is why I want to tell you our story." In 1942, Helen was a child in Northern France when her homeland was invaded by Nazi Germany. Just eight years old, Helen mostly concerns herself with school and being best friends with Lydia. With the Nazi occupation comes a law that all Jews must wear a yellow star on their clothes, something Helen and her best friend Lydia, who must wear the star, do not fully understand.

On the eve of Helen's ninth birthday, Lydia comes for a celebratory overnight visit. On that same night, the Nazis begin to round up all Jews, and in her desire to be with her own parents, Lydia asks to go home. Helen is hurt by Lydia's departure and regrettably shouts that Lydia is no longer her friend.

Helen never sees Lydia again, and never knows—even after the war ends—what became of her cherished friend and her parents. Because she never has the chance to tell Lydia that she was her very best friend, that she regrets her anger that night, Helen eventually transforms her grief for Lydia into hope. She longs for the day they might see one another again.

Severe with their angular geometry and ponderous black outlines, the austere illustrations powerfully capture the harsh gravity of the subject matter. A dull, almost lifeless palette mirrors the atrocities the Nazis committed as they systematically murdered nearly six million Jews. Text and art in this picture book invite readers to imagine Lydia's personal anguish, which in turn makes it feasible for readers to begin to conceive of the collective suffering of six million lives.

Suggested Activities

- Have the students compare the two very different picture books about the Holocaust: *Let the Celebrations Begin!* (Orchard, 1991), written by Margaret Wild and illustrated by Julie Vivas; and *Rose Blanche* (Creative Editions, 1985), written by Roberto Innocenti. Discuss why some books about the Holocaust have "happy endings." Ask the students to decide what audiences the two books are appropriate for by looking at their pictures and words; their judgments should reflect a critical evaluation of the books, based on principles of excellence previously discussed, about character, plot, theme, and style.
- Have older students view Steven Spielberg's movie *Schindler's List,* as well as some documentaries about the Holocaust. Allow students ample time to discuss their personal responses to the movies. Decide as a group what further aspect of the Holocaust the students will study.

• Imagine that Lydia and her family escaped safely to a neutral country. Create a correspondence between Lydia and Helen, sharing letters the two best friends wrote each other for a year.

• Present a dramatic skit of Lydia's and Helen's reunion many years later, when each of them is a grandmother; over dinner, the two could catch up on their lives. Present it to another class.

• Search on the Internet for any websites on the Holocaust; create a bulletin board of reproductions of some primary sources from the Holocaust; discuss and analyze them. If possible, invite a Holocaust survivor to speak to students, or write to one, with carefully considered questions included in your letters.

The Wall

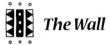

Eve Bunting. 1990. *The Wall.* Illustrated by Ronald Himler. New York: Clarion. ISBN 0-395-51588-2

Synopsis

Eve Bunting has written over 150 books in an amazing range of genres and for readers of all ages. Born and schooled in Northern Ireland, Bunting has crafted realistic fiction that often deals with poignant social issues. She tackles illiteracy, homelessness, aging grandparents, and riots in U.S. cities. Her topic for this inimitable picture book is war and its aftermath. In *The Wall,* Bunting's writing is perceptive and powerful; when paired with Ronald Himler's expressive watercolor illustrations, the result is simply unforgettable.

The dramatic narrative begins with this book's cover: Readers see a young father with his own young son perched atop his shoulders as the two face the Vietnam Veterans Memorial in Washington, D.C. The story—credibly told from the young child's point of view—describes their visit to the national monument that honors those patriots who perished in the Vietnam War. They have come to the wall that is "black and shiny as a mirror" to find the name of the boy's grandfather, who is only one among the fifty-eight thousand listed.

The boy observes other visitors: an amputee in a wheelchair; an older man and woman weeping inconsolably; a chatty class of older schoolgirls on a field trip; and, a grandfather enjoying a walk with his young grandson. Father and son find Grandpa's name and make a rubbing of it to take home as a memento. They leave a school photograph of the child on the grass below in a sea of souvenirs that includes flowers, tiny U.S. flags, and beloved stuffed animals.

The wall itself is present in every picture in the background. Shades of gray color the stone monolith, aptly echoing the complexities of the war for which it stands. Himler's evocative watercolor illustrations remind readers that this story was crafted with tears for the deaths of loved ones killed in war, as well as for the sacrificial love of one's country.

Suggested Activities

- Have students interview any Vietnam veterans who reside in the community; invite that person or persons to come and discuss their experiences. Anthologize the interviews into a classroom collection to share with other classes studying the Vietnam War.
- Study other national monuments and memorials found in Washington, D.C., and have groups of students prepare presentations about each of them. Find out when these monuments and memorials were erected, what they honor, who created them, and who visits them. Arlington National Cemetery, the Lincoln Memorial, and the Marine Corps War Memorial (Iwo Jima statue) are just a few.
- Let the class construct several student-made jackdaws (photocopies of historical printed matter such as newspaper articles, letters, journal entries, maps, photographs and the like) containing artifacts that a young U.S. soldier might have had in his or her possession during a stint in Vietnam. Maps of Cambodia, letters from loved ones, photocopies of newspaper articles of the time, and so on, might be included.
- Research the resistance to the Vietnam War, learning about the lives of those Americans who did not want the country involved in that conflict. Pick five important personages who became famous for their outspoken

ways; write biographies of their lives. Create a collage of people, songs, books, and actions that stood for the antiwar movement associated with the Vietnam War; display it prominently in a school hallway.

- Learn about other famous walls throughout history—the Wailing Wall, the Great Wall of China, and the Berlin Wall—that have both good and bad effects. Create a bulletin board display that shares the students' findings. Some students may want to create three-dimensional models of these historically famous walls.

For Further Reading

Adler, David. 1995. *One Yellow Daffodil: A Hanukkah Story.* Illustrated by Lloyd Bloom. San Diego: Harcourt Brace. A lonely but compassionate Holocaust survivor, a florist named Morris Kaplan, accepts the friendship of two young siblings, who also help him rekindle his religious beliefs. The book's evocative paintings reinforce this gentle look at the lingering aftermath of war.

Bunting, Eve. 1998. *So Far from the Sea.* Illustrated by Chris K. Soentpiet. New York: Clarion. During the 1970s, a Japanese American family returns to an ancestor's gravesite—Manzanar—where Japanese living in the United States were interned during World War II. The visit helps seven-year-old Laura clarify war's complexities and celebrate her grandfather's love for his adopted homeland. Sepia-toned watercolors alternate with colored illustrations to contrast the past and present.

Coerr, Eleanor. 1993. *Sadako.* Illustrated by Ed Young. New York: Putnam. 1993. An unforgettable story, with illustrations dominated by muted pastel tones, describes the young child Sadako's courageous struggle with leukemia, a fatal illness caused by the atomic bombing of Hiroshima during World War II. Inspired by the author's classic novel and the film based on it.

Heide, Florence Parry & Judith Heide Gilliland. 1992. *Sami and the Time of the Troubles.* Illustrated by Ted Lewin. New York: Clarion. Ten-year-old Sami lives in a basement shelter in Beirut, where civil war rages unabated, his entire homeland torn apart by violence, destruction, and death. Each emotionally charged watercolor illustration expresses Sami's resolve to live until a time "when the fighting has stopped."

Innocenti, Roberto & Christophe Gallaz. 1985. *Rose Blanche.* Translated by Martha Coventry and Richard Graglia. Chicago: Creative Editions. A young German girl living near a concentration camp reaches out compassionately to the inmates she sees there, an action that leads ultimately to her own death. The powerful, graphic illustrations lend unsettling details to this somber Holocaust story.

Lee, Milly. 1997. *Nim and the War Effort.* Illustrated by Yangsook Choi. New York: Farrar, Straus, & Giroux. Nim, a young patriotic citizen living in San Francisco's Chinatown during World War II, wins the paper drive her school sponsors. A lesson from her grandfather also makes her proud of her Chinese American heritage and marks her real triumph.

Mochizuki, Ken. 1993. *Baseball Saved Us.* Illustrated by Dom Lee. New York: Lee & Low. A Japanese American boy remembers life imprisoned in an internment camp during World War II, where his one salvation, ironically, was to play baseball, the American pastime. Somber-hued, textured paintings capture the bleakness of the desolate environment and convey the struggle of individuals who maintain human dignity and self-respect despite adversity.

Weitzman, David. 1997. *Old Ironsides: Americans Build a Fighting Ship.* Boston: Houghton Mifflin. A ship carpenter's son narrates a fictionalized account of the construction of America's revered warship, the U.S.S. Constitution. Intricate pen-and-ink drawings capture every detail of the building of this magnificent sailing vessel.

Chapter 2

By Word of Mouth

Traditional Literature

> Picturebooks—books intended for young children which communicate information or tell stories through a series of many pictures combined with relatively slight texts or no texts at all—are unlike any other form of verbal or visual art. . . . [T]hey exist primarily so that they can assist in the telling of stories.
>
> —Perry Nodelman, *Words About Pictures*

Technically known as traditional literature, folklore is among the most popular and memorable of all genres. Primary-grade teachers in particular love this body of literature, having used fairy tales and folktales extensively in their classrooms for the past decade. Because it has been the province solely of primary-grade children and their teachers for such a long time, most intermediate-grade teachers quickly dismiss fairy tales and folktales as nothing they could share with their older, more sophisticated classes.

I beg to differ. Folklore in picture book form is an important and exciting body of literature for all ages. My classroom experience using traditional literature with older students has convinced me that the genre, especially when presented in picture books, is extremely well suited for children in the intermediate grades. The reasons are compelling and easy to enumerate.

First, most older children are already quite knowledgeable about folktales collected and transcribed centuries ago by such literary scholars as the Frenchman Charles Perrault and the Brothers Grimm from Germany. Such familiarity provides fertile soil for the seeds of fractured versions of these stories to grow and flourish for the specific enjoyment of older, sophisticated readers. Jon Scieszka and Lane Smith's *The Stinky Cheese Man and Other Fairly Stupid Tales* (Viking, 1992) is perhaps the most successful of all these fractured tales. Intermediate-grade students love the irreverent humor, rollicking absurdity, and lighthearted spoofery in parodies like *Stinky Cheese;* they revel in their own fractured retellings or contemporary adaptations.

Second, older readers can usually identify the characteristics of classic folklore: simple structure; progressive, fast-moving plot; stock characters; lively action; repetition of chants; and succinct endings. Older readers will readily find these characteristics in more recent variations and be able to see the interconnectedness among all traditional forms of storytelling throughout the world.

Finally, studying and reading traditional literature motivates older students to engage in meaningful writing activities that often result in delightful twists of familiar versions, fascinating "what if. . .?" situations regarding traditional tales, or entirely original creations of legends, myths, and tales. With their own words and pictures, intermediate-grade children can create original stories that continue to attempt to explain their world.

The titles highlighted here will please older readers and their teachers alike: a mirthful, fractured retelling of the well-known Rumplestiltskin; a Cambodian trickster tale; a comical, surprisingly contemporary Mongolian folktale; a classic Andersen tale all dressed up in "brand new clothes;" and lastly, a West African folk story that urges all living things to coexist harmoniously.

Rumplestiltskin's Daughter

Diane Stanley. 1997. *Rumplestiltskin's Daughter.* New York: Morrow. ISBN 0-688-14327-X

Synopsis

In this hilarious spoof, creator Diane Stanley provides older readers with genuinely irreverent tongue-in-cheek. Empowering her text with a contemporary sensibility and poking great fun at visual references in her pictures, Stanley turns the classic Grimms' fairy tale topsy-turvy. The result? Golden!

In Stanley's version, Rumplestiltskin wants to *adopt* the miller's daughter's firstborn child. He declares: "I promise I'll be an excellent father. I know all the lullabies. I'll read to the child every day. I'll even coach Little League." Meredith—that's the miller's daughter's name—likes what she sees in this fatherly figure. She also admits a penchant for short gentlemen. So the two marry and together live a quiet country life together far from the king's palace.

When their only child, a sixteen-year-old daughter, aptly named Hope, ventures out "to see more of the world," she finds herself facing the same impossible task her mother encountered earlier: spinning straw into gold for the very same greedy monarch. Using her wits, Hope outsmarts the avaricious leader, betters his kingdom, and becomes the country's benevolent, happily single prime minister.

Full-color illustrations, rendered in gouache, colored pencil, and collage, portray bug-eyed caricatures of all the characters and outfit the king with a wild wig and wacky wardrobe. The abundant use of the color gold provides comic relief aimed at the greedy king. In the banquet hall where a "sumptuous feast" has just been served, viewers glimpse at gold platters, golden candelabras, gold eating utensils, gold-studded table and chairs, and the King himself cleaning his teeth with a golden toothpick. A wealth of humorous details, such as the parodies of portraits that hang on the castle walls, is certain to elicit giggles and guffaws from older students and teachers alike.

Suggested Activities

• Find as many fractured retellings of traditional fairy tales in picture book form as you possibly can: Steven Kellogg's *The Three Little Pigs* (Morrow, 1997), Susan Lowell's *The Bootmaker and the Elves* (Orchard, 1997), and Richard Egielski's *The Gingerbread Boy* (HarperCollins, 1997) are among the noteworthy entrants in the genre. Compile a bibliography and a list of the characteristics you think make up such spoofs. Using your list, decide whether or not your selected tales are successfully retold and illustrated. Create wall murals of your "picks" and "pans."

• On the C.I.P. information page and on the dedication page in Stanley's book are two delightful postcards that Hope had written to her parents about her situation at the king's. Have the students create their own postcards home to Hope's mom and dad, illustrating one side and writing a brief letter on the other. Hang them from the classroom ceiling on fish line, which allows for viewing of both sides.

• Have students choose other classic fairy tales and write sequels or continuations to the already well-known stories. Encourage children to play with locale, modifying the point of view, or giving characters attributes that are opposite their traditional traits (the little, kind wolf).

• Present a dramatization of Stanley's *Rumplestiltskin's Daughter*. Be creative with the props and costumery. Or create a skit in which a television reporter like Barbara Walters interviews Hope Machengeld, the kingdom's new prime minister. Perform it for parents and caregivers.

Brother Rabbit: A Cambodian Tale

Minfong Ho & Saphan Ros. 1997. *Brother Rabbit: A Cambodian Tale*. Illustrated by Jennifer Hewitson. New York: Lothrop. ISBN 0-688-12552-2

Synopsis

Famous folklore characters such as Brer Rabbit and Anansi the Spider find another quick-witted, fleet-footed critter in their trickster midst: He's

Cambodia's Brother Rabbit, and he uses his guile and impudence to outsmart bigger and more powerful characters, such as a sharp-toothed crocodile, two elephants, and a village woman. Set in the farm fields and small villages of Cambodia, the folktale recounts several instances in which plucky and cheerful Brother Rabbit gets the better of his would-be aggressors, much to readers' satisfaction.

Brother Rabbit connives the hungry crocodile into ferrying him across a river to partake in a feast of delicious rice seedlings. He feigns death to a woman hungry for a curried rabbit dinner, and hitches a ride in the banana-laden basket atop her head as she goes to market, eating all the fruit and escaping in the nick of time. He then lures an angry mother elephant into helping him detach from a pitch-covered tree stump, to which his tail is stuck fast. All in a day's work!

All of Brother Rabbit's mischievous deeds add dramatic tension to this engaging tale, and further endear him to sympathetic readers. Also dramatic and engaging are Hewitson's striking illustrations. Rendered in watercolor paints and ink, they resemble the brightly colored batik fabrics that originate from Cambodia, and ably invest the story with a tone of cultural authenticity. Detailed notes at the book's beginning discuss the long and impressive history of the rabbit motif in the country's oral tradition. The authors compare Brother Rabbit to the people of Cambodia, who have, in the everpresent face of wartime adversity, exhibited pluck, resilience, and sheer determination.

Suggested Activities

- Study numerous countries to learn of the different kinds of animals that tell these cultures' trickster tales. Research the folktales of England, Scandinavia, Germany, Mexico, Africa, Native America, France, China, Japan, and Russia. Make a wall-sized chart of your findings; include drawings of these animals from around the world.
- The authors' foreword mentions that traditionally Cambodian tales were presented through history in the form of folk plays. Recast *Brother Rabbit* as a play and present it to a primary-grade audience. This could also be performed as a shadow-puppet play.

• Have students write the further adventures of Brother Rabbit, which should include the small, clever main character turning the tables on a stronger, dim-witted adversary. Include colorful illustrations and compile the writings and pictures into a classroom book.

• Have students create a story map of Brother Rabbit's encounters with the other characters in the folktale. Compare Brother Rabbit's pattern of situations to the patterns found in Van Dyke Parks' and Malcolm Jones' *Jump! The Adventures of Brer Rabbit* (Harcourt Brace, 1986), or Gerald McDermott's *Zomo the Rabbit: A Trickster Tale from West Africa* (Harcourt Brace, 1992).

• *Watership Down* (Macmillan, 1974), by Richard Adams, makes a superlative read-aloud for an older audience and may provide fodder for lively discussion as to why the rabbit is often chosen as the central character in trickster tales. In *Watership Down,* look closely at its great chief rabbit and trickster, El-ahrairah, who creates many of the rabbit civilization's myths and legends. Compare his character to others mentioned earlier.

The Khan's Daughter

Laurence Yep. 1997. *The Khan's Daughter: A Mongolian Folktale.* Illustrated by Jean and Mou-sien Tseng. New York: Scholastic. ISBN 0-590-48389-7

Synopsis

Flowing text and spirited pictures mark this amusing adaptation of a Mongolian folktale delightfully retold by Newbery Honor Book author Laurence Yep. Möngke, a "bumpkin" of a shepherd boy, wants his father's prophecy to come true: that Möngke will some day be the husband of the wealthy Khan's daughter. "To seek his bride," the simpleton travels to the city where the royal family resides. The Khan's shrewd wife demands of Möngke three daunting tasks in an attempt to ridicule and embarrass him.

Pure luck allows Möngke to perform successfully the first two tests of strength and bravery. He cannot pass the final trial of wisdom, which is actually a clever guise orchestrated by the Khan's daughter. Möngke's actions, however, convince the young woman that he will be "a prudent husband who won't get himself killed at the first opportunity." The two marry and live "contentedly for the rest of their lives."

Full of wry humor, the story also contains a rather contemporary moral as it demonstrates that fairness and equality are traits deserving of both men and women. Gold, in prodigious amounts, colors border frames and ornamental motifs, found in Mongolian art; it lends the book an exotic atmosphere. Handsome watercolor illustrations further enrich the tale's foreign setting by distinguishing cultural details but also serve to convey the genuine comedy of this very funny noodlehead tale.

Suggested Activities

- The title page displays a picture of a Mongolian horse-head cello, an instrument that storytellers often played to accompany their oral tales. Have a group of students prepare a research report about this instrument; share it with the class.
- Locate the country of Mongolia on the globe; draw a map of it. Discover information about its people, its history, and its culture. Make a bulletin board that displays the students' findings.
- Have students write original noodlehead stories, choosing the United States as the setting. Include three tasks that their character must perform to achieve his or her goal. Students will illustrate their own stories. Display finished tales in the school library.
- Prepare a special meal that includes Mongolian fare. If possible, invite a chef versed in preparing such food to come and speak to the class.
- In the story, there are seven demons that Möngke defeats. Have seven students create their own artwork of these monsters, making them as unique as possible and in keeping with the type of illustrations that are found in the book.
- Find another noodlehead tale from another culture; have students make a comparison chart of the two folktales as they examine likenesses and differences among characters, events, themes, and motifs found in each of them.

The Emperor's New Clothes

Hans Christian Andersen. 1997. *The Emperor's New Clothes.* Translated by Naomi Lewis. Illustrated by Angela Barrett. Cambridge, Massachusetts: Candlewick Press. ISBN 0-7636-0119-5

Synopsis

With its simple, honest words, Naomi Lewis' superb translation of one of Hans Christian Andersen's most widely recognized literary fairy tales will enchant a host of older readers. And, with grand panache, Angela Barrett's luxurious paintings provide a visual richness that adorn the story spectacularly and will likewise lure curious observers. Together, text and art fashion a truly charming picture book that is ingenious and breathtaking.

Readers familiar with the storyline will notice the newly infused humor and its contemporary touch. Also updated, by virtue of the splendid illustrations, is the tale's elegant setting: the time, pre-World War I; the place, a small coastal European principality. They are the perfect combination to present the classic story of the obsessively fashionable monarch who ultimately refuses to be bested by two roguish weavers.

Richly detailed and strikingly designed, the book invites perusal. Older children will delight in period pictures of the fancy Hispano Suiza motor car, and one of a biplane, too. The king's *haute couture* wardrobe includes stylish robes, skiing outfits, tailcoats, cruiseware, and "a different coat for every hour of the day." Barrett adds hilarious touches as she includes a pack of equally chic dogs sporting jewels and fluffy bows. Her highly colorful palette, with its profusion of purples, suggesting royalty, and its pinks lend a fanciful air to the book and its underlying message (which is anything but fanciful). Older readers will easily sense the folly of trusting other people's impressions and know that, for this wise emperor, the naked truth will reign.

Suggested Activities

- In an extensive foreword, the translator poses a question: Would Andersen, who wrote this story in 1837, have approved of the newly transposed setting? Divide students into two groups and debate the question.
- The imagined setting is similar to that of Monaco in 1913. Research this tiny country: What was the kingdom like then? What is it like today? Display student findings on a wall mural, using a time line and pictures to share information.
- Pick another famous Andersen tale, perhaps *The Snow Queen, The Little Mermaid, Thumbelina,* or *The Ugly Duckling.* In your own words, write a retelling of the story; provide your own illustrations. Make a classroom book that contains all of the retellings.
- Find out about the life of the Danish poet and writer, Hans Christian Andersen, who created original folktales in traditional form. Share an oral report with the class about the person who wrote over 150 literary fairy tales. Include as many primary sources as possible.
- Find three other picture book editions of *The Emperor's New Clothes.* Compare translations of the text, and illustrations as well. Chart similarities and differences. Encourage students to create their own versions of this tale, using a 1990s, American background. Pay particular attention to the wardrobes the main characters will wear.
- Research the maxim "Clothes make the man"; share your findings with the class; argue for or against believing in the adage.
- Look at some Scandinavian folktales that were collected in the early 1840s by Peter Christian Asbjorsen and Jorgen Moe. Read several picture book editions of "East of the Sun and West of the Moon," among the most famous of these stories.

The Hunterman and the Crocodile

Baba Waguè Diakité. *The Hunterman and the Crocodile: A West African Folktale.* New York: Scholastic Press. ISBN: 0-590-89828-0

Synopsis

This lively folktale from West Africa, where the oral tradition has been a highly developed art for thousands of years, emphasizes "the importance of living in harmony with nature and the necessity of placing Man among—not above—all living things."

The story begins when Bamba the Crocodile and his family travel by way of land on a pilgrimage to Mecca. Their energies and food supplies run short, and when Donso the Hunterman passes by, Bamba the Crocodile pleads with the hunter to help by carrying his family to their home in the deep river waters. Skeptical at first, a foolish Donso agrees, and afterward finds his hand trapped between the hungry Bamba's powerful jaws.

A cow, a horse, a chicken, and an old mango tree refuse to rescue Donso the Hunterman because of what Man has done to them. A clever trickster rabbit, however, is responsible for Donso's turn of good fortune. Donso finally learns that Man's peaceful cooperation with Bamba the crocodile and all the other plants and creatures is important and necessary in life.

Diakité's bold and vibrant illustrations provide remarkable companionship to his simply told tale; they are testament to the fact that he is a consummate story artist as well as talented storyteller. His stylized black figures, with their white outline against a bright orange background, are prominently displayed on unique ceramic-tile paintings. Their narrative content says as much about the story as do the words.

Also impressive is Diakité's masterful and plentiful use of a white background throughout the entire picture book. An interesting author's note sheds personal light on the significance of traditional storytelling to this native West African, and includes the titles of other similar versions of this delightful tale.

Suggested Activities

- Have students retell the entire folktale in pictures only; let them paint their illustrations on ceramic tiles—made from self-hardening clay or purchased at a craft store—just as the author–illustrator did for the book. Display them on the wall.

• Choose to read one of the variants of this folktale mentioned in the book; make a comparison chart of the similarities and differences between the two tales; what can you learn about the different cultures from which these two stories come?

• Have the children create masks depicting the various characters and perform a creative drama of the folktale. Retain the West African flavor of the story by drawing similar motifs you find in the illustrations. Create your own play program with similar borders found in the pictures. Photocopy and distribute these to the audience.

• Make a papier-mâché model of your favorite character in the folktale. Paint it, using the same bold color palette. Display it in your school library.

• Research the flora and fauna that are native to Mali, West Africa; learn if any species of animals or plants and trees are endangered or extinct; tell why each is endangered; find out what people are doing to help save this animal or plant. Share your findings in chart form with accompanying pictures.

• Invite to your class a parent or member of the community who has traveled to a country in West Africa. Have the adult present a slide lecture, bring in currency from that country, come in African dress, or bring additional African art or jewelry. Conclude with ample time for student-generated questions and lively discussion.

For Further Reading

Aardema, Verna. 1997. *Anansi Does the Impossible!: An Ashanti Tale.* Illustrated by Lisa Desimini. New York: Atheneum. Distinctive mixed media collages unite with the rhythm of the true storyteller's voice to celebrate how trickster Anansi the spider, acting on advice from his sagacious wife, reclaims his people's stories from the powerful Sky God.

Ben-Ezer, Ehud. 1997. *Hosni the Dreamer: An Arabian Tale.* Illustrated by Uri Shulevitz. New York: Farrar, Straus, & Giroux. A shepherd journeys from the desert to a bustling city, where he pays one gold dinar for the wise words that enable him to find love and prosperity;

jewel-like hues and ample white backgrounds delineate characters and setting.

Manna, Anthony L. & Christodoula Mitakidou. 1997. *Mr. Semolina-Semolinus: A Greek Folktale.* Illustrated by Giselle Potter. New York: Atheneum. Combining almonds, sugar, and semolina, Princess Areti concocts her ideal mate—"five times beautiful and ten times kind." Colorful pencil and ink illustrations lend additional silliness and humor to this popular Mediterranean folktale.

McDermott, Gerald. 1997. *Musicians of the Sun.* New York: Simon & Schuster. A superb rendition of an ancient Aztec myth that pits Wind against Sun; the star holds the musicians Red, Blue, Yellow, and Green captive. The oversized format showcases brilliant artwork executed in oil pastel and acrylic fabric paint applied to handcrafted Mexican paper.

Meddaugh, Susan. 1997. *Cinderella's Rat.* Boston: Houghton Mifflin. Recounted by a rat transformed into one of Cinderella's coachmen, this hilarious spoof offers older readers much to laugh about through its spirited, fractured text and dancing cartoon line drawings.

Pollock, Penny. 1996. *The Turkey Girl: A Zuni Cinderella Story.* Illustrated by Ed Young. Boston: Little Brown. A Native American variant of the well-known tale that emphasizes one's relationship with nature and the importance of keeping promises. Dramatic drawings in oil crayon and pastel represent the indigenous hues of the desert Southwest.

Van Laan, Nancy. 1998. *The Magic Bean Tree: A Legend from Argentina.* Illustrated by Beatriz Vidal. Boston: Houghton Mifflin. A well-researched story and colorful folk-art gouache illustrations celebrate a young Argentinian boy's intrepid quest to the magical carob tree in the "middle of the wide pampas" to save his beloved country from a deadly drought.

Zelinsky, Paul O. 1997. *Rapunzel.* Retold and illustrated by Paul O. Zelinsky. New York: Dutton. In this 1998 Caldecott Medal winner, opulent oil paintings reminiscent of the Italian Renaissance accompany the retelling of the familiar story, the written version of which dates back to Italy in the 1600s.

Chapter 3 Beyond Shel and Jack

Poetry

> [A picture book] is like a good poem. You shouldn't be aware of the pastings together. A picture book has to have that incredible seamless look to it when it's finished.
>
> —Maurice Sendak, *Caldecott & Co.: Notes on Books and Pictures*

Several educational studies have found that between the third and fifth grades, many classroom children become disinterested in poetry. Some experts go even further and suggest that intermediate-grade teachers are to blame, accusing them of destroying children's inherent love for this body of children's literature. I contend that this alienation is largely due to middle-grade teachers' misunderstandings about what children's poetry is, and so they misuse it with their students. I further maintain that poetry in the form of picture book editions might well be part of the panacea for rekindling middle schoolers' enthusiasm for enjoying and learning about this genre.

For more than two decades, preeminently popular poets Shel Silverstein and Jack Prelutsky, in their breezy, irreverent fashions, have produced children's poetry that has skyrocketed students' interest in the genre. *Where the Sidewalk Ends: Poems and Drawings* (Harper, 1974), *The Light in the Attic* (Harper, 1981), *The New Kid on the Block* (Greenwillow, 1984), and *Something BIG Has Been Here* (Greenwillow, 1990) are arguably the most recognized anthologies of poetry found in schools today. Teachers, too, have loved these books, and continue to rely on them to "teach" poetry.

The point I want to emphasize is this: In addition to these four reliable volumes are scores of other notable works of poetry in picture book form. These books are certain to help intermediate-grade teachers recreate positive climates for their students to celebrate poetry, not only in the aural realm (the music they hear with their ears), but also in the visual realm (the images they see with their eyes).

How can teachers revitalize their students' involvement in poetry? The first golden rule: Just relax and share spontaneously a variety of poetry with your class every single day. And what better way to accomplish that goal than by sharing poems found in picture books! In a handful of minutes, from start to finish, children can listen to *and* look at the beauty of illustrated poetry. Just as the publishing world has recently begun creating superb single-book editions of folktales, fairy tales, and songs, it has likewise, in an effort to integrate text and art, followed suit in poetry. I am duly impressed at the extraordinary number of these exceptional picture books that have been published in the last two or three years.

The second golden rule: select picture book poetry that genuinely reflects children's tastes in the genre; acknowledge their likes and dislikes, and immerse students in a variety of verbal and visual activities that involve their preferences. Poetry is really best when heard and seen daily; children need to be amused, delighted, and engaged consistently with both of these aspects of poetry. Middle-grade students will enjoy listening to and looking at poetry when teachers afford them opportunities that offer them the chance to do just that.

Finally, invite students daily to imagine, compose, revise, publish, illustrate, and share their own poetry. Celebrate student-created works within your classrooms; I assure you, you *and* your children will be the richer for it. I have highlighted four picture books of poetry that I believe are remarkably well suited for use in middle school classrooms. They include an eloquent book of months, full of imagistic language and stunning illustrations; a clever takeoff of a popular counting folksong ingeniously pictured; a lively collection of poems commemorating school valentines and love notes; and a verbal and visual tribute to the game of basketball.

January Rides the Wind: A Book of Months

Charlotte F. Otten. 1997. *January Rides the Wind: A Book of Months.* Illustrated by Todd L. W. Doney. New York: Lothrop. ISBN: 0-688-12556-5

Synopsis

Verbal artistry in the form of rich sensory images makes this collection of a dozen brief poems that celebrate the months of the year fresh and scintillating. Strikingly simple free verse captures each month's essence, employing many of the elements of poetry that classroom teachers may easily discuss with their students. All twelve poems are equally lyrical and delightfully musical when read aloud.

In tribute to the last month, the poet writes: "December runs to darkness, / shortens days, / stretches night to night, / stockpiles badgers, bears, and bats. . . / holds its breath for spring." The brevity of the verses will likely convince students that less is more, while at the same time allow for easy identification of the metaphors, similes, alliteration, internal rhymes, and word repetition that abound throughout the poems.

Luxuriant oil paintings, in oversized double-page spreads, accompany the poetic text and reflect a visual craftsmanship that is truly spectacular. The luminescent illustrations ably depict the lush green of April, the harvest gold of September, the wintry gray of February. Not only do the colorful paintings echo the seasonal transformations the plant and animal worlds undergo during the course of the year, they also narrate the goings-on of a multicultural troupe of children happily engaged in the variety of year-round outdoor activities. Well-chosen, compact words combine with sumptuously textured illustrations; together they create a breathtaking picture book of poetry—just perfect for intermediate-grade students' enjoyment.

I've listed a few more activities than usual, only because I think that *January Rides the Wind* is exactly the kind of picture book that, on first impression, may be quickly dismissed as not holding much potential for intermediate-grade classroom use. On the contrary, I envision that this slim little volume could actually provide the framework for an exciting yearlong study of poetry, one that would amuse, delight, and engage youngsters in this type of literature. I think it would serve quite well as the touchstone book for a formal introduction to the elements of poetry.

Suggested Activities

• At the start of the school year, have students find a plot of land—this could be chosen on school grounds or near a student's home—that contains flora and fauna. Once a month, students will draw detailed sketches of their plots and record, in written paragraph form, all of their observations. Monthly sketches and written observations may be placed on a special bulletin board. At the end of the school year, compile all of a student's nine entries into a booklet format that shows the seasonal cycle of each student's plot. Share among classmates, discussing similar and different observations; display the collection in the school library.

• Have sets of partners choose a special object from their plots of land as the topic for a poem. First have them sketch the object, providing as much detailed accuracy as possible. Next, have them generate a list of vocabulary words that appropriately describe their object. Finally, using both the illustrations and the list, have them write a poem about their object.

• Using the names of the months, have students write acrostic poems that, in their minds, capture the seasonal essence of each month's characteristics. They should also provide accompanying tempera paintings for their poetry. Display these in sequence on a classroom wall.

• Have middle school students choose two months that represent contrasting times of the year. Students will write their own diamante poetry and provide illustrations. Take time to present these projects in an attractive manner; diamond-shaped pieces of drawing paper for the student illustrations are dramatic and aesthetically pleasing.

• Have students discover and list all of the specific animals mentioned in each of months' poems; from the list, have them choose one animal about which to write an expository report. In their findings, have students follow their animals throughout the entire year, noting changes in the animals' habitats, appearance, diet, and so on.

• Invite a fine artist, perhaps a landscape oil painter, to come and speak to the classroom students. Have that artist bring the equipment necessary to produce completed works of art, and also have him or her share painterly techniques by way of a demonstration. As a culminating event, plan a field trip to a local fine arts gallery.

• Have the students survey the entire school to see in what months children in all of the grades were born; graph the results using bar, line, and circle graphs that are large enough to be put on display in hallways.

The Halloween House

Erica Silverman. 1997. *The Halloween House.* Illustrated by Jon Agee. New York: Farrar, Straus, & Giroux. ISBN: 0-374-33-270-3

Synopsis

An ingenious takeoff on a well-known folksong provides the poetic structure for this waggishly illustrated Halloween story. Silverman's unique reversal of "Over in the Meadow" begins, "In the Halloween house, / in a dark, dingy den. . . / a papa werewolf crouched / with his little ones ten." Besides howling werewolves there are rising vampires, squirming worms, swooping bats, dancing skeletons, and a host of other haunting nocturnal creatures who vanish at daybreak the following morning.

Providing most of the humor, however, are Agee's playful, lively, pen-and-ink line drawings rendered in appropriately dusky colors. The illustrations unfold yet another story within the story, depicting two convicts on the lam, wearing merrily striped garb, who seek overnight shelter in the haunted hideout. The pair are fearfully chased from room to room by the assorted ghouls, just managing to escape alive and willingly return to the safe, homey comforts of their prison cell.

The jovial cartoon characters—prisoners and ghastly inhabitants alike—are certain to give readers more delight than fright. This picture book is pure fun, and its clever textual twist will serve as an ideal model to get middle-grade students started in creative poetry writing.

Suggested Activities

• Have the students compile a collection of takeoffs; each student should select a different one for this anthology, and all takeoffs should be illustrated. Also include the original poems or songs that were altered in the process of creating the takeoffs. This book should be displayed in the school library for all to enjoy.

• Many children love creative dramatization and its natural connection to poetry. Have small groups of students choose a favorite takeoff poem to reenact; include as many student-made props as possible; perform for other language arts classes, perhaps for a class comprised of younger Buddy Readers.

• Create a "Barney" program that parodies the introductory song for that popular television children's show. Have students work in small groups; collectively they can write their own takeoffs; share these with the entire class.

• Have students look for picture book editions of single poems or folksongs. Make a collection of these to create a poetry corner in the classroom. Honor student choices rather than books that are selected only by the teacher. You might want to include a listening center as well, where students can listen to accomplished poets read their works, or where they might be able to record their own oral interpretations of poetry.

Love Letters

Arnold Adoff. 1997. *Love Letters.* Illustrated by Lisa Desimini. New York: The Blue Sky Press/Scholastic. ISBN: 0-590-48478-8

Synopsis

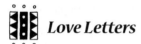

With its epistolary text, this collection of twenty poems praises the joys and delights expressed in valentines, school notes, and love letters addressed to classmates, parents, siblings, pets, and even enemies. Written by the critically acclaimed poet Arnold Adoff, this slim volume also contains captivating illustrations by creative picture book artist, Lisa Desimini. Richly textured collages, sculptured clay models, color photographs, and oil paintings are among the variety of media she employs; all techniques represent a coquéttish interpretation of these fun-loving messages.

The title page offers readers a winsome, visual delight: On a large, traditionally familiar valentine card, replete with lacy, delicate white paper doilies that scallop the edge of a construction-paper red heart, sparkles the name of the volume. Displayed in gold-glittered letters across the handcrafted creation, the book's name echoes the scintillating emotions that the messages inside contain, as well as reinforces the notion that the notes come from the most important part of their readers—their hearts. A vibrant, purple background quickly reminds senders, however, that most of all, a fanciful insouciance prevails throughout the collection, making most of the valentines unabashedly humorous and imaginatively pleasurable.

Chockful of rhythmic vitality, Adoff's verses are also visual treats, with their trademark playful arrangement of words on each page. His strategic placement of those words allows readers to focus on them, ponder them, and to enjoy them as an emphatic part of the poem. Adoff's wide variety of odes include valentines to a classroom crush from an anonymous admirer; to a nurturing, cookie-baking, candy-making, grandmother from a grateful grandchild; and affectionate exchanges to and from siblings.

With his charming poems, Adoff quietly celebrates the idiosyncratic charms of both sender and receiver; with her whimsical illustrations, Desimini inimitably incarnates the gamut of heartfelt emotions the verses extol. Both poet and artist infuse the spirited collection with a *joie de vivre* that make this volume a heartsome, welcome addition to the enjoyable study of poetry.

Suggested Activities

- For Valentine's Day, assign students the task of composing a valentine poem to a family member; they should be thoughtful about incorporating into their poems one loving aspect of their relationship with that special relative. Have them include a mixed-media collage illustration with their poem.
- This volume of poetry serves as an excellent introduction to an author study of Arnold Adoff. Research the poet's life, education, and career. Find as many volumes of his poetry as you possibly can; establish an Arnold

Adoff library in a classroom corner. Discuss Adoff's work to discover any central themes that perhaps run throughout all of his books. Adoff also has a website and does author visits; check it out.

- Make a classroom collection of children's books that use collage for their illustrations. Some collage artists include Esphyr Slobodkina, Eric Carle, David Wisniewski, David Diaz, Giles Laroche, Steve Jenkins, Denise Fleming, and Lisa Desimini. Make a comparison chart of these illustrators' similarities and differences. Invite the art teacher in for a specialized lecture on this medium; culminate with each student creating an original piece of collage art.
- Have students write secret admirer notes in riddle form. They should provide subtle but accurate clues about who the sender is; display the riddle notes on a classroom bulletin board. Have students guess the writers' identities. Celebrate divulging who the secret admirers are by distributing to the entire class those candy hearts with brief messages printed on them. Enjoy!

Hoops

Robert Burleigh. 1997. *Hoops*. Illustrated by Stephen T. Johnson. San Diego: Silver Whistle/Harcourt Brace. ISBN: 0-590-48478-8

Synopsis

In this brief, poetic ode to the game of basketball, the author celebrates the kinesthetics that come alive on the court. Using the fewest words, Burleigh paints action-packed images of the skills and plays the opposing players exhibit: "The never-stop back and forth flow, / like tides going in, going out." These players not only move, they "glide, swerve, slip, roll, lurk, and leap" in impassioned acts of pure energy.

The compact, free verse also contains powerful alliterative phrases—"The feathery fingertip roll and soft slow drop"—which glide off one's tongue as effortlessly as the basketball moves among the players' deft hands. There is a rhythmical quality to the poem, which echoes the pulse of the bouncing ball, and it yearns to be shared out loud.

With vigorous, dynamic pastel chalk drawings, Caldecott Honor artist Stephen T. Johnson perfectly matches Burleigh's vibrant text. The first double-page spread, a chainlink fence in its background, suggests that this game may be enjoyed outdoors, in scrimmage fashion, inviting anyone to partake. Many illustrations of the players are cropped dramatically, revealing only parts of athletic bodies, and imply that these players have far too much energy to harness within the confines of the book's pages. On the players' faces, readers observe the determination, stamina, and dedication that these young people, men and women alike, bring to the sport.

A handsome design sense informs the picture book with an equal vitality that also mirrors the game's lifeblood. The oversized, white typeface of the text, set in black, boxlike shapes, is randomly placed on each of the pages, and imitates the bounce of the ball itself. With its exciting topic, energetic artwork, and ebullient text, this picture book poem clearly wins with older readers.

Suggested Activities

- Research the origins of the game of basketball. Who invented it? When and where was it first played? Trace the chronology of the sport to the present day, and discuss the current global popularity of the game. Share your findings with the class in illustrated time line form.
- Have students select another sport that will serve as inspiration for them to compose their own poems. Discuss the need to choose words carefully, words that express the essence of their game. Possible topics are football, baseball, tennis, soccer, rugby, ice hockey, gymnastics, figure skating, downhill skiing, and track and field.
- Brainstorm for a list of professional basketball superstars. Have students work in small groups, with each group selecting a famous player to research; be sure to include childhood, high school, college, and professional experience. Be prepared to discuss personality traits of the star, and whether he or she serves as a good role model for young children. Display report findings on a classroom bulletin board.

• Compare Robert Burleigh's *Hoops* with Bruce Brooks' picture book, *NBA by the Numbers* (Scholastic, 1997). Make a comparison chart of the similarities and differences between the two books. Discuss how information about the game of basketball is presented in each; look at strengths and weaknesses of each book.

• Invite the local high school basketball team for an informational session with your classroom. Have students prepare appropriate questions beforehand that they want to pose to the group.

• Make a classroom dictionary comprised of basketball lingo. Some entries might include *brick, slam dunk, downtown, swisher,* and so on. In addition to clear, concise definitions, include illustrations.

• Watch the documentary *Hoop Dreams* and talk about ambition, direction, and the likelihood of a person realizing a professional basketball career.

For Further Reading

Asch, Frank. 1998. *Cactus Poems.* Photographed by Ted Levin. San Diego: Harcourt Brace. This collection highlights an assortment of plants and animals found in the four North American deserts. Full-color photographs ably celebrate the magnificence and wildness of this remarkable ecosystem.

Bryan, Ashley. 1997. *Ashley Bryan's ABC of African American Poetry.* New York: Atheneum. The alphabet provides the framework for this anthology of poems—some fragments, some complete—by renowned poets, including Cullen, Hughes, Greenfield, Giovanni, and Dunbar. Bryan's tempera and gouache paintings masterfully complement the selections.

Florian, Douglas. 1998. *insectlopedia: poems and paintings.* San Diego: Harcourt Brace. In this companion to *beast feast, on the wing,* and *in the swim* (all from Harcourt Brace), Florian crafts twenty-one brief poems about such insects as termites, crickets, and ticks. Watercolors painted on brown paper bags combine with collage to add whimsy and exuberance.

Ho, Minfong. 1996. *Maples in the Mist: Children's Poems from the Tang Dynasty.* Illustrated by Jean and Mou-sien Tseng. New York: Lothrop. Translated from the Chinese, this compilation contains sixteen traditional Tang Dynasty children's poems, written over one thousand years ago. Chinese calligraphy and classic watercolor illustrations evoke an exotic sentiment throughout this handsome collection.

Hopkins, Lee Bennett. 1997. *Marvelous Math: A Book of Poems.* Illustrated by Karen Barbour. New York: Simon & Schuster. Vibrant gouache and acrylic paintings complement a lighthearted selection of sixteen poems, which demonstrates—with words—how numbers are an integral part of our daily lives. Mary O'Neill, Lillian M. Fisher, and Karla Kuskin are among the versifiers represented.

Kennedy, X. J. 1997. *Uncle Switch: Loony Limericks.* Illustrated by John O'Brien. New York: McElderry. Original limericks describe a day in the life of eccentric Uncle Switch, a "turned-around man" who does everything topsy-turvy. Finely cross-hatched line drawings infuse this odd-ball character with humor and absurdity.

Sandburg, Carl. 1998. *Grassroots.* Illustrated by Wendell Minor. San Diego: Harcourt Brace. These fourteen poems by our national poet pay homage to America's Midwest and praise the heartland's many treasures, including prairie skies, summer corn, and October sun. Majestic watercolors enhance the beautifully distilled language.

Swann, Brian. 1998. *Touching the Distance: Native American Riddle Poems.* Illustrated by Maria Rendon. San Diego: Harcourt Brace. Original adaptations of riddles from sundry Native American tribes, these fourteen short poems are accompanied by equally original, colorful mixed-media collage illustrations that divulge the answers to the conundrums.

Chapter 4 Other People's Lives

Biography

> In picture books the drawings, of course, are as important as, or more important than, the text. . . .[T]he text can only give bones to the story. The pictures, on the other hand, must do more than just illustrate the story. They must elaborate it.
>
> —Edward Ardizzone, *Only Connect: Readings on Children's Literature*

During the last decade, the picture book biography has deservedly and prominently found an increasingly wide audience among older readers. Thoroughly researched, factually accurate, authentic, believable, and engaging stories about the life of a real person accompanied by illustrations can accelerate a meaningful journey into the past. The 1984 Caldecott Award winner, *The Glorious Flight: Across the Channel with Louis Blériot, July 25, 1909* (Viking, 1983), written and illustrated by Alice and Martin Provensen, exemplifies this idea.

This picture book biography is a gem. The Provensens' illustrations depict so clearly the series of events and the character of the individual that led to the successful flight across the English channel that we feel as though we were there, right beside Monsieur Blériot, every step of the way. These pictures, with their dramatic shifts of perspective, heighten the reader's awareness of the eminent risk involved in attempting to fly an airplane across the English Channel in 1909.

Authentically detailed paintings also quickly establish an acute sense of time and place. Women don elaborate hats and tote parasols; men drive nascent automobiles right next to men who ride horse-drawn carts. Such images, though never mentioned in the text, verify this period in history and contribute to the reader's grasp of when and where the momentous event transpired.

Picture book biography illustrations provide far more than that which older children learn by reading the text alone. Words do tell dates and places. But visual details reveal pertinent information about those times and places: What did people wear? In what kinds of houses did they live? What kinds of places did they work in? At what kinds of pictures did they look? What kinds of food did they eat? What kinds of animals did they keep as pets—or meet in the wild? What was the climate like?

Second, illustrations infuse life into the personage as they help the reader shape the character into a distinct human being. The pictures give face to that someone. Eyes, mouth, brow, and jaw: All of these may divulge to a reader a substantial amount about the person's character, intangible qualities that may not be mentioned in the text. Finally, illustrations in picture book biography lend verisimilitude: If successful, they convince the reader that a particular person really and truly lived.

The four picture books highlighted in this chapter embody all of the customary literary and artistic evaluative guidelines. They stand as shining examples of exceptional picture book biographies. Readers will discover, through fine storylines and artful pictures, how other people have lived their lives. With their informative texts and elucidating illustrations, these picture book biographies would likely have impressed our old friend Johann Comenius, who knew the educational power of linking the image with the word.

The first book examines the life of one of history's most creative individuals. The second chronicles the life of a visionary nonconformist, a brilliant scientist misunderstood by the political hierarchy of his time. The third recounts the childhood of the man who became synonymous with his people, the Sioux. The last presents the life of the son of a slave who became the world's most famous African American rodeo star.

Leonardo da Vinci

Diane Stanley. 1996. *Leonardo da Vinci.* New York: Morrow.
ISBN: 0-688-10437-1

Synopsis

In a masterful marriage of text and illustration, Diane Stanley offers older readers a trenchantly interesting account of the talents and shortcomings of one of the Renaissance's—and perhaps all history's—most gifted geniuses. In her introductory note, Stanley elucidates that inimitable time period known as the Renaissance, during which da Vinci lived. This gives readers a helpful time line and essential background information in which to place da Vinci's life story.

Beginning with da Vinci's illegitimate birth in 1452 in Florence, Italy, Stanley chronicles Leonardo's early childhood and the apprenticeship of his teen years to a famous artist. She ably recounts his adult life, when, in search of a sustaining patron, da Vinci worked for dukes, kings, and popes. Extraordinary artist that he was, da Vinci was also an amazing inventor, clever engineer, brilliant scientist, human anatomist, and voluminous writer.

At the age of thirty, da Vinci began putting down his thoughts and ideas in notebooks; for the next thirty-seven years he continued to fill the pages of his notebooks with incredible sketches, plans, and observations, filling literally thousands and thousands of pages. Penning all of these notebooks in a unique backward script, da Vinci sometimes wrote using a secret code.

Stanley also honestly discusses da Vinci's propensity to abandon projects, often leaving paintings unfinished. In doing so, she offers readers a well-balanced portrait of this immensely talented man, which makes him all the more human. Her inclusion of da Vinci's foibles alongside his talents makes for a totally realistic portrayal of this genius' life, which ultimately permits readers to know the subject as a real person.

Stanley includes reproductions of actual drawings from da Vinci's notebooks, cleverly placing them on each of the text pages. She also frames both words and notebook fragments in exquisite borders, made up of a series of gold knots; they are adaptations from a design by da Vinci. Her own artwork, a combination of watercolor, gouache, colored pencil, and photo collage, captures the brilliance of da Vinci's many gifts. She further includes facsimiles of the most famous of da Vinci's paintings, *Mona Lisa* and *The Last Supper.*

In an equally engrossing postscript, Stanley relates the fate of da Vinci's notebooks; thousands of pages are still unaccounted for. The scholarship behind Stanley's words and the integrity of her pictures make Leonardo da Vinci's story come to life; it is a remarkable survey that older students will find irresistible.

Suggested Activities

• Have students imagine that several hundred pages of da Vinci's notebooks have recently been uncovered. Write a newspaper article that discusses the particulars and accompany it with pictures of the sketches that were found. Be creative, drawing an "invention" that da Vinci himself might have thought of.

• Hold a paper airplane–flying contest. Plan for several categories for this event. Some suggestions: whose airplane flies the greatest distance; whose airplane is the most creatively designed; whose airplane stays in the air the longest; and so on.

• Leonardo da Vinci wrote from right to left and backwards; try writing messages in this fashion and discover whether any students can decipher them without the aid of mirrors. Invent your own coded script; offer messages to classmates to see if any can decipher the code.

• Invent your own machine, tool, or gadget. Include a detailed drawing of your invention and a written explanation of exactly what it will do; give it a name. Make a prototype of your gadget; share all inventions in a classroom display. Take this one step further and invite a local attorney versed in patent law to describe the procedure of patenting a new product or invention. Submit patent applications for his or her review. For further information, write to the United States Patent and Trademark Office, U.S. Department of Commerce, Washington, D.C. 20231.

• Look at other picture book biographies that Diane Stanley has crafted. *Bard of Avon: The Story of William Shakespeare; Charles Dickens: The Man Who Had Great Expectations;* and *Shaka, King of the Zulus* (all from Morrow) are a few. Have the students evaluate them. Look specifically at how the information of the person's life is conveyed: Are there strengths and weaknesses portrayed? How so? How do they differ from those in *Leonardo*? Students may want to create language charts or Venn diagrams to share their findings.

- Invite a portrait artist to come to the class. Have that person lecture on the technique that da Vinci himself discovered: *chiaroscuro* and *contrapposto.* Provide time to research the *Mona Lisa*; share your findings in a report. Culminate the unit of study with a field trip to a local fine arts gallery or museum.
- By the way, E.L. Konigsburg's *The Second Mrs. Giaconda* (Aladdin/Simon, 1988) makes for a terrific read-aloud when learning about da Vinci. Utilizing her trademark creative license, Konigsburg explains from the perspective of Salai, the servant, how his master, da Vinci, painted the *Mona Lisa.*

Starry Messenger: Galileo Galilei

Peter Sis. 1996. *Starry Messenger: Galileo Galilei.* New York: Farrar, Straus, & Giroux. ISBN: 0-374-37191-1

Synopsis

I think Peter Sis is a master at crafting picture books, many of which I consider perfect. One of his more recent endeavors, this book is a shining example of how words and illustrations interact to create an extraordinary picture book biography.

Starry Messenger is the life story of the iconoclast Galileo Galilei, a "famous scientist, mathematician, astronomer, philosopher, and physicist." In simple and understated language, Sis begins, "In the city of Pisa, a little boy was born with stars in his eyes. His parents named him Galileo." Galileo shattered the prevailing belief that the earth was not the center of the universe, and because of such thinking, eventually paid dearly with his loss of freedom. The unadorned, straightforward text honestly unfolds Galileo's courageous tale of daring—to challenge staid ideas and not follow tradition. Sis' illustrations, however, are anything but unadorned and straightforward.

Extreme complements to Sis' simple story, the intricately elaborate illustrations are chockfull of so much to pore over that readers could spend hours just examining them. Hatched and cross-hatched, these exquisitely detailed fine-line drawings add rich texture for viewers. Visual delights include helpful time lines, meticulous maps, exacting borders, and miniature vignettes. Galileo's own profound quotations, often scripted by Sis in his hand-written cursive, sometimes meander delightfully about each page; they further bolster that visual texture and make for provocative reading.

One especially telling illustration depicts a young Galileo and literally hundreds of other children engaged in whimsical play with each other. Galileo, however, stands out distinctively among the crowd, with a stick in hand, scratching bright blue stars in the earth-toned dirt. This use of blue, and the liberal amounts of blue and yellow throughout the entire book, capably evoke the celestial mood of the sky and stars that are almost always in Galileo's thoughts.

This stunning picture book biography will lure older readers to its inviting pages time and time again. It not only informs them about the life of Galileo, it may also inspire them to observe their world through a visionary lens, one that lets them see the joy of discovery.

Suggested Activities

- Ask your school librarian to locate a video on Galileo. View it with your students. Have students compare and contrast how the information is presented in both forms. To chart their findings, a Venn diagram will prove helpful as a graphic organizer.
- In *Starry Messenger,* Galileo makes some astute scientific observations about the moon. Have the students record their own observations of the moon for an entire month; sketch daily the different phases of the moon. Have them learn the meanings of these moon phases: new, crescent, quarter, gibbous, and full.
- Galileo also had some original thoughts regarding our sun. Break into small groups and research a particular aspect of the sun. Possible topics might include sun spots, dangers of too much exposure to the sun, how hot the sun is, and solar eclipses.

- Find a copy of the picture book biography, *Galileo* (Macmillan, 1992) by Leonard Everett Fisher. Compare and contrast the two editions, looking critically at the strengths and weaknesses present in the books. Chart your findings.
- Using *Starry Messenger: Galileo Galilei* as your resource, create a wall mural that chronicles Galileo's life story. Include a time line at the bottom of your mural; display it in the library media center.
- Check out a copy of Myra Cohn Livingston's book of poetry entitled *Space Songs* (Holiday, 1988). Recite the poems to another class that is studying astronomy; have students create poster-sized illustrations to accompany the various poems presented.
- During the course of a themed unit on astronomy, generate a class list of appropriate vocabulary words on chart paper. Working in pairs, have students create their own crossword puzzles using those words. Photocopy the puzzles; compile them in booklet form, one for each student.
- Imagine a brand new constellation. Name it, draw its configuration, and create a story that explains how it came to be known. Have students share orally the origin of their constellations. Compile their work into book form as well.
- As a culminating activity, arrange for a class field trip to a nearby planetarium, or plan for a star-gazing evening to which students and their families may come.

A Boy Called Slow: The True Story of Sitting Bull

Joseph Bruchac. 1994. *A Boy Called Slow: The True Story of Sitting Bull.* Illustrated by Rocco Baviera. New York: Philomel.
ISBN: 0-399-22692-3

Synopsis

Native American storyteller and poet Joseph Bruchac gracefully and perceptively shares the childhood story of the most recognized Lakota Sioux chief and medicine man the United States has known: Sitting Bull. Bruchac's superb storytelling is linked with illustrations so vivid that the reader feels transported almost instantly back to the vast prairies and endless plains the Lakotas called home.

Born "in the winter of 1831" to a family belonging to the Hunkpapa band of Lakota Sioux, Sitting Bull was first given the childhood name—as was the custom—*Slon-he,* or Slow, because he was "careful and deliberate" in his actions. Young Slow listens to the stories shared by his extended family, and as he listens, he learns much about the ways of his people.

Throughout his boyhood, Slow yearns for a different name, a good and strong one like his father's, Returns Again to Strike the Enemy, or that of his uncle's, Four Horns. Slow longs for the day when he might act bravely and wisely on behalf of his people and therefore earn a new, and respected, name. Despite his frustration, he thrives during his early years and becomes known for his broad, strong shoulders and his skill at riding horses, earning admiration from the other young boys.

One wintry night, a fourteen-year-old Slow accompanies his father and some other Hunkpapa tribesmen as they raid a nearby, threatening Crow war party. With full courage and resolve, Slow takes command and leads the Lakota attack, forcing the Crow warriors to flee in defeat. Proud of his son's valor and determination, Slow's father then gives his son a new and noteworthy name: *Tatan'ka Iiyota'ke,* which means Sitting Bull.

Bruchac deftly tells this important life story with words that recall the oral tradition. Because many sentences begin with *so* or *and*, readers quickly gain a sense of "listening" to this life story, rather than simply reading it. And, when read aloud, its sounds as if a living voice is very casually sharing the tale. One can almost imagine a story like this one being told to young Slow himself. Bruchac's word choice is simple, his style is direct, and his voice is distinct; all combine to create Sitting Bull's dramatic coming-of-age life story.

Illustrator Rocco Baviera skillfully renders heavily textured, full-color paintings in a misty, atmospheric palette that give shape to Slow and his life story. Along with shades of earthen brown, midnight blue, and dusky gray, Baviera also surprises and delights viewers with occasional bold splashes of vibrantly bright hues of dazzling purple, fiery orange, and luminous yellow. Note especially the first illustration: In the picture's top right-hand corner, readers get a bird's eye view of a slender crescent moon alight in a vivified, plum-colored sky dotted with wintry white snowflakes; in the upper left-hand corner, one discerns a vague outline of a sagacious owl sitting wide-eyed in the branch of a tree; on the ground below stand the numerous Lakota tipis, all dark and shadowy except for one. From it emanates a warm, golden glow, commemorating the birth of a boy called Slow. Throughout the book, similar striking color contrasts also produce the drama and energy that mark this extraordinary rite of passage tale and help to enliven Sitting Bull's life narrative.

Suggested Activities

- This suggested activity comes from Bruchac himself; I found it in his extremely resourceful *Tell Me a Tale: A Book About Storytelling* (Harcourt Brace, 1997). Bruchac mentions a storytelling bag that Abenaki and Iroquois storytellers sometimes carried with them to use when an audience gathered round, eager to listen to a tale. In the bag were various small objects: a crow's feather, an arrowhead, a porcupine's quill, and so on, each of which represents a story. Have students create a classroom storytelling bag—made from woolen felt tied with a leather thong—and then fill it with small, unbreakable items that are good for starting stories. Students then "reach in and pull out a story" by selecting an item from the bag. Give ample time—three or four days—for students to create original stories: Porquois tales, trickster tales, or talking animal tales are just a few they might consider. Share stories with students seated in a circle.
- Have each student uncover an original family history story, one that has actually happened to someone; prepare to share it orally; culminate the activity by holding an all-class storytelling day. Invite special guests such as the administrator, the librarian, and the superintendent of schools (and, of course, invite your local newspaper reporter).
- Have students create for themselves their own special descriptive names, ones that they feel embody a certain quality that each of them possesses. In a one-page essay, the students will write about the ways that demonstrate the appropriateness of the names they have selected. Compile the essays in a class book to share with other classes.
- Bruchac's biography includes no research notes, offers no sources for his story of Sitting Bull, yet still rings true. Have a small group of students

research Sitting Bull's life story. Check Bruchac's version for authenticity and veracity. Share your findings by creating a large Venn diagram that compares and contrasts the two different versions.

- The last of the Indian wars in the West was in 1890 at Wounded Knee, the time and place where Sitting Bull died. Unearth the specifics of what happened then and there, namely the massacre of the Sioux Indians. Select three or four students to prepare an oral report; have them share their findings with the entire class.
- Where do you presently reside? Discover who lived on that land three hundred years ago. Display your findings on a wall mural or timeline that depicts the various changes. Working in small groups, think of some alternative plans that could have allowed the Native Americans and the New Americans to inhabit the land together peacefully.
- Create a classroom picture book biography of yet another young Sioux child, who was given the name "Pitiful Last" at birth, earned the name Ohiyesa—which means "The Winner"—when he grew to adulthood and was also known as Charles Eastman. Born in 1858, this amazing person was brought up by the Plains Indians, attended Dartmouth College and Boston University, and eventually became a respected physician, lawyer, and writer. Strive for an authentic, lively text; pair that with informative illustrations. Share with another class that is also studying Native Americans in American History.

Bill Pickett: Rodeo-Ridin' Cowboy

Andrea D. Pinkney. 1996. *Bill Pickett: Rodeo-Ridin' Cowboy.* Illustrated by Brian Pinkney. San Diego: Gulliver Books/Harcourt Brace. ISBN: 0-15-200100-X

Synopsis

For the past several years, the husband-and-wife team of Brian and Andrea D. Pinkney has been collaborating on the creation of praiseworthy picture book biographies about remarkable African Americans. The author and illustrator duo have masterfully produced such titles as *Alvin Ailey* (Hyperion,

1993), and *Dear Benjamin Banneker* (Harcourt, 1994), which was recognized as a Notable Children's Trade Book in the Field of Social Studies. Their collaborative efforts to make *Bill Pickett: Rodeo-Ridin' Cowboy* are equally impressive.

Andrea Pinkney deftly establishes the colloquial tone for Pickett's fascinating life story by beginning first with a poem that hints at the greatness of this man's tale: "Yeah, folks been tellin' the tale / since way back when. / And they'll keep on tellin' it / till time's time ends." Brian Pinkney perfectly authenticates the text with a sepia-toned photograph taken of the rodeo star atop his horse. Picture and poem immediately engage readers, compelling them to turn the page for the rest of the story.

The second of thirteen children, Willie M. Pickett was born around 1860 to once-enslaved parents, who settled north of Abilene, Texas, prior to the Civil War. Growing up on his mama and daddy's farm, Bill (as he was called) eschews agrarian ways, dreaming "of the day when he'd be old enough to rope mossback cattle and help stray dogies keep up with the herd."

It's as a young boy that Bill one day spies a bulldog biting firmly on the bottom lip of a skittish cow, calming the animal. Convinced that he can learn that trick, Bill does just that. "Invented there and then by feisty Bill Pickett, that was bulldogging, bite-'em style." As Bill grows, so do his talents as a cowhand. News of his skilled and fearless horsemanship spreads quickly through Texas, where Bill finally gets to perform his bulldogging trick in a large rodeo arena.

He gains fame instantly and is invited to perform his bulldoggin' at rodeos throughout the West, as well as distant places such as Madison Square Garden in New York City, Mexico City, Canada, South America, and even in England for the King and Queen. Wherever he goes, folks call him the Dusky Demon "on account of the dusty dirt cloud that billowed behind him" as he bulldogs those cattle down. Bill Pickett is famous throughout the world.

Brian Pinkney's signature scratchboard renderings, hand-colored with oil paints, smartly adorn cream-colored pages. The paper's ecru hue reinforces the organic, close-to-the-earth feel this very special life story possesses. Pinkney's bright palette includes a blazen sky-blue, lush greens, and organic browns. Curvilinear, fluid lines effortlessly corral the movement and energy of adventurous cowboys, bucking horses, and restless cattle, as well as ably depicting the West during a time when it was still called "Wild."

Small vignettes—one in particular shows a trail crew sitting comfortably around a blazing campfire, "with nobody watching them but the stars"—are winning complements to the numerous double-page spreads that depict expansive skies, seemingly endless plains, or Bill as a "young'un," as he intrepidly leaps from horse to steer only to perform his astonishing bulldogging feat.

An interesting afterword contains additional information about the historical significance of African American cowboys during the United States' western movement, as well as an explanation of the origin and development of the rodeo. A comprehensive bibliography further bolsters the fact that the book's text was exceedingly well researched. This one, folks, is an exceptionally entertaining read, and an absolute must for your students.

Suggested Activities

- Imagine yourself as Bill Pickett, away on one of your trips, touring with the rodeo circuit. From each of the exotic places you travel, write postcards addressed to your wife and children, telling them about your bulldogging performances and the sights and sounds of the country you are visiting. Use sturdy Bristol paper and make certain the postcards are large enough—and appropriately illustrated on the reverse side—to display from your classroom ceiling.
- In her bibliography, Andrea Pinkney lists Edgar R. Potter's *Cowboy Slang* (Golden West, 1986); obtain that title, or one similar, to aid in creating a classroom dictionary or alphabet book that contains some of the colorful language the cowboys used. Make it oversized and illustrate it. Display it in an all-school media center.
- Tod Cody's (a descendant of William F. Cody) *The Cowboy's Handbook: How to Become a Hero of the Wild West* (Cobblehill/Dutton, 1996) is another invaluable resource. It contains a recipe for cooking up a "mess" of three-bean chili and a host of other cowboy activities.
- From an art supply store, purchase scratchboard paper. Have students create scratch drawings, inspired by the westward movement, onto the paper; add subsequent color with watercolor paints. Display these in the classroom or hallway for passersby to admire. Rather than one big rendering, you might want to consider a series of smaller vignettes for this project.

• With assistance from the music education teacher, obtain suitable arrangements of traditional cowboy songs. "Git Along, Little Dogies" is only one example I found in *From Sea to Shining Sea* (Scholastic, 1993); "The Streets of Laredo" is another. Accompany singing voices with some students playing guitars and autoharps. Memorize all songs to perfection in preparation for a cowboy concert. Dress in western garb for the official performance; present it to parents and family members during an evening concert.

• The text mentions that the *Wyoming Tribune* and the *Denver Post* printed stories of Bill Pickett's bulldoggin' talents. Pretend you are a reporter and write a newspaper account of Bill's story for one of these newspapers. Remember, "the newspapers didn't seem to care if Bill was black or white—Bill's *bulldogging* was news!" Include rich and colorful language; illustrate your newspaper article and display it on a classroom wall.

For Further Reading

Bedard, Michael. 1997. *Glass Town.* Illustrated by Laura Fernandez and Rick Jacobson. New York: Atheneum/Simon & Schuster. Told from young Charlotte Brontë's perspective, this unconventional fictionalized biography provides a look into the quotidian events of her literary family's exceptionally unusual life. Striking gothic oil paintings of remote English moors aptly convey a sense of place.

Bradby, Marie. 1995. *More Than Anything Else.* Illustrated by Chris K. Soentpiet. New York: Orchard. Poignant, heartfelt words and luminous watercolor paintings work in concert to create a fictionalized biographical account of a particular time in the childhood of a singular American hero: Booker T. Washington, who toils "from sunup to sundown," but dreams of becoming "the best reader in the country."

Cooney, Barbara. 1996. *Eleanor.* New York: Viking. Rich in period detail and emotionally intense, this intimate portrait of the lonely but privileged childhood of Eleanor Roosevelt provides significant insight into the life of one of the most remarkable women of the twentieth century.

Cooper, Floyd. 1994. *Coming Home: From the Life of Langston Hughes.* New York: Philomel. Cooper's trademark full-color, highly textured oil paintings punctuate the partial biography that shares the childhood dreams and longings of the African American who later became one of the Harlem Renaissance's most revered poets.

Krull, Kathleen. 1996. *Wilma Unlimited: How Wilma Rudolph Became the World's Fastest Woman.* Illustrated by David Diaz. San Diego: Harcourt Brace. Accompanied by illustrations in mixed-media collage and brightly hued paintings, the simple narrative presents the deeply inspirational life story of the African American woman who courageously triumphed over monumental physical challenges to become an Olympic heroine.

McPhail, David. 1996. *In Flight with David McPhail: A Creative Autobiography.* Portsmouth, NH: Heinemann. Creator of nearly fifty books, McPhail sprinkles childhood photographs, favorite characters, and reproductions of actual dummies throughout this insightful memoir. From his inception of an idea to completed product, he divulges many aspects of the creative process.

Spivak, Dawnine. 1997. *Grass Sandals: The Travels of Basho.* Illustrated by Demi. New York: Atheneum Books for Young Readers. An abbreviated version of the chronicle of the journeys taken by the beloved seventeenth-century Japanese poet Basho, a man remembered for his creation of timeless haiku. Detailed Oriental paintings, Japanese calligraphy, and original poetry adorn each two-page spread.

Stanley, Diane & Peter Vennema. 1994. *Cleopatra.* Illustrated by Diane Stanley. New York: Morrow Junior Books. Gouache paintings, executed in elaborate mosaics, and thoroughly researched, lucid prose mark this compelling life story of one of history's most remarkable women: the intelligent, powerful, wealthy, and truly visionary Queen of Egypt, Cleopatra.

Chapter 5 Science Is a Way of Knowing

Nonfiction

> If I contribute to this thing called Knowledge, it is because I encourage and insist that our brains and eyes remain continually in touch with each other.
>
> —David Macaulay,
> *The Zena Sutherland Lectures*

We live in an informational age, infused with a wealth of scientific knowledge that changes daily. Because of this phenomenon, many educators throughout the United States have begun to reexamine the sometimes obsolete, often ineffective method they have used exclusively in their formal instruction of science: the traditional textbook. Some teachers at the vanguard have vocalized opposition to the use of these textbooks alone to inform students of the natural sciences. They have opened their minds and hearts to recent nonfiction picture books to teach science.

Many of these visionary teachers have also eschewed the trite notion of demanding that their students memorize trivial data and mindless, isolated fragments of knowledge. Instead, they want their charges to become adept at comprehending the concepts that provide the basis of our scientific world; they value a "process versus product" approach.

The classroom teachers champion the sharing of nonfiction picture books to implement what they believe to be one of the most essential components of teaching science today: to instill in students a sense of wonder that nurtures the curiosity they inherently possess about their world. I find it especially exciting, because these kinds of science teachers are rapidly growing in conviction and in number!

Teaching science to older readers by using nonfiction trade books in picture book format rather than textbooks offers students many compelling advantages. First, and foremost, picture book texts may reflect a wide range of reading abilities. They are especially suited for classrooms in which grade-level reading disparities exist among students; nearly any student can find a picture book on a particular scientific topic that contains words and illustrations appropriate for his or her reading level. Textbooks fall miserably short in this arena, often being written above grade level for most students!

Second, because picture books are published annually, they contain the most recent scientific information. Textbooks, on the other hand, which may be purchased by school districts once every ten years, simply cannot keep as current with cutting-edge findings and discoveries in science. Brand new picture books about today's newfound knowledge—and it's so important that these books be new—offer students up-to-date information, and at a fraction of the cost of textbooks for an entire district.

Third, nonfiction picture books may represent scores of perspectives regarding their scientific subject matter. This variety of viewpoints provides readers with books that contain a global introduction to a particular topic and may serve as a springboard for further study. Other picture books may offer more detailed, focused looks at the same subject, which is ideal when students delve deeper into their topic as they search for more sophisticated information. Textbooks, on the other hand, usually share with their audience a broad, general, singular viewpoint. Consequently, their information seems shallow, basic, and myopic.

Finally, picture books about science offer visually literate students a plethora of opportunities to learn much from their illustrations. Superlative photographs, detailed illustrations, and friendly, informative graphics—all of these extraordinary images let students observe and increase their grasp of scientific knowledge in a concrete form, in much the same way that our fellow teacher Comenius recognized and promoted among children more than three centuries ago!

The first picture book I offer delineates the fascinating physical characteristics of one of earth's most precious resources—water. The second provides an insouciant introduction to Roman numerals, as it celebrates that mathematical concept in a unique, aesthetic fashion. The third poignantly commemorates the plant and animal life of the North American prairie, one of the earth's most magnificent ecosystems. Using a question-and-answer format, this last book discusses all aspects of bats. All four picture books exhort the exploration of science in fresh, new ways; together with words and pictures, these books increase older readers' understanding and pleasure.

A Drop of Water: A Book of Science and Wonder

Walter Wick. 1997. *A Drop of Water: A Book of Science and Wonder.* New York: Scholastic. ISBN: 0-590-22197-3

Synopsis

Walter Wick combines crisp, arresting photographs with a brief, pellucid text as he pays remarkable tribute to the substance that covers three-fourths of the earth's surface—water. In an oversized format that contains simple words and splendid photographic illustrations, Wick elucidates many of water's dazzling physical characteristics: Surface tension, condensation, capillary action, and evaporation are among the properties highlighted. Visual and verbal interpretations reveal the fascinating transformations that water undergoes as well; readers learn much about water in the form of ice, snowflakes, frost, and dew.

In one particular image, Wick's camera magnifies a snowflake sixty times its actual size. In this photograph, readers view an enormous seven-inch crystalline flake dramatically set against a brilliant blue background. The image convinces admirers that such beautiful, detailed intricacies of this natural creation are second to none.

Wick then pairs the magic of that artistic image with a page of text that scientifically explains snowflake formation. Water molecules, in extremely cold air, he writes, will adhere to a particle to make a tiny ice crystal. And, as "more water molecules from the air freeze onto the crystal, they join at angles that allow a six-sided structure to form." Illustration and words are integral to the knowledge shared; it is as interesting to look at as it is to read.

Turn the page to observe a dozen varieties of equally wondrous, enlarged snowflakes; they represent the endless number of shapes and sizes in which snowflakes may fall to the ground. Wick also cleverly shows the same twelve snowflakes in their actual sizes, which offers readers a graphic comparison that is easily understood.

Besides magnifying images, Wick's camera sometimes freezes action to disclose some of water's physical properties. In "Molecules in Motion," a sequence of nine captivating photos demonstrates what happens to a drop of blue-dyed water when it's added to a jar of plain water. The result is truly lovely to see. And, when Wick complements this aesthetic visual with a gracefully written exposition of the scientific process of moving molecules, the result is truly easy to understand.

A science book of this kind deserves attention and recognition; small wonder that it received the prestigious 1997 Boston Globe–Horn Book Award for Nonfiction. And exactly what kind of science book is it? I think Wick states it best in his award acceptance speech: "It occurred to me that I could make a science book for children from a perspective I knew best—concrete, direct observations of scientific phenomena through photographs."

Suggested Activities

- Wick's book includes an engaging afterword that invites young scientists to learn more about water by participating in their own "careful observation and diligent experimentation." The suggested activities are the perfect follow-up for a classroom of science students and include experiments with soap bubbles, making rainbows, and floating paper clips, to name just a few. So comprehensive are Wick's last three pages, a science teacher using them could feasibly plan for his or her class an entire unit of study about water!

• I also include an assortment of my own ideas and activities: Arrange for a class field trip to your local water-treatment plant. After the visit, create a wall mural that depicts the various stages of purification you observed at the treatment facility. Display the mural in a hallway.

• For all classes at your grade level, hold a poster contest that emphasizes important water conservation measures that can be adopted by informed citizens. Ask three or four employees from your water treatment plant to judge the posters for originality and message. Award the winner with a case of bottled drinking water.

• Obtain your school building's water bill for one month. Analyze data such as cost and amount of water used during a one-week period. Launch an all-school effort to reduce the number of gallons of water usage for one week. When the bill comes for that particular period, compare the two different weeks' results in a line graph.

• Have a small group of students research the waterways that run through or surround your town; discover how clean they are at present, how polluted they might have been in the past, and what efforts have ever been made to clean up the water. Prepare your findings in a report to share with the entire class.

• Create and prepare a skit intended for the primary grades that encourages some important water conservation practices that they can implement. Make your cast of characters appealing to young children: Drip, Drop, and Plop are suggestions for three original characters.

• Obtain from the music teacher a recording of George Handel's *Suite from the Water Music*. (MCA Classics has produced one such recording by the Royal Philharmonic Orchestra, with Yehudi Menuhin conducting). Have the students listen to the suite to serve as inspiration while they create original watercolor artwork. Display the artwork in the music room.

• Write to Save Our Streams, Adopt a Stream, Isaac Walton League of America, 707 Conservation Lane, Gaithersburg, MD 20878; or call 800-284-4952 for information that might help protect local waterways. Have the entire class—or school—adopt a stream.

Roman Numerals I to MM: Liber De Difficillimo Computando Numerum

Arthur Geisert. 1996. *Roman Numerals I to MM: Liber De Difficillimo Computando Numerum.* Boston: Houghton Mifflin.
ISBN: 0-395-74519-5

Synopsis

Only picture book creator Arthur Geisert, through his masterful command of the classic art of etching, achieves such verve and energy with meticulous, sculptural lines. Only Arthur Geisert infuses his picture books with a dry, witty sense of humor that elicits chuckles and chortles. And, only Arthur Geisert would pair concrete objects such as tiny, charming, pink pigs—now his trademark—with the abstract concept of Roman numerals, to create an incredibly ingenious picture book just perfect for older readers.

With a laconic, subdued text, Geisert introduces the requisite cast of basic symbols—I, V, X, L, C, D, and M—that constitute the Roman numerals. It is with porcine profusion, however, that he comically illustrates his understated text, using porkers as counters to let readers determine the value of each Roman number!

Three small vignettes on a single page equate I with one piglet, V with five, X with ten, and so on. To depict how many pigs D stands for requires more space—a double-page spread, in fact. The rural landscape background reveals a hillside swimming hole filled with pale, blue water surrounded by faded olive-green grass. A handful of cottonwood trees, some bearing twisted trunks and gnarled branches, dots the hilltop.

The content of the foreground, however, is far more delectable: a bounty of five hundred piglets, colored the prettiest pale pink imaginable. In the bottom right-hand corner, a half dozen pigs frolic in and on a staved barrel. To their left, twenty pigs snuggle cozily for an afternoon nap. Behind the barrel acrobats stand another six pigs atop a huge tree stump. And there's only 468 others left to count!

In the pond, there are pigs cavorting on floating logs, pigs dog paddling, pigs swimming the sidestroke, pigs diving, pigs in mid-air, and pigs slip-sliding into the water on wooden planks. Literally hundreds of other pigs cluster the hillside. Some mill about; others saunter nonchalantly. All are having fun. The double-page spread that enumerates—as the book's title promises—MM piglets will likely impress readers most of all.

Further discourse explains that any and all integers may be combined and written by following two rules that dictate adding or subtracting the Roman numerals, depending on their position and placement. The playful pigs illustrate this notion, too, as twenty more of Geisert's vignettes demonstrate counting from I through XX.

Five remaining double-page illustrations provide trenchantly interactive practice for novices who really want to become proficient with the Roman numerical system. These remarkably detailed etchings offer readers additional counting exercises, and more. So strong are the pictures' storytelling qualities, the images give readers tales to ponder and also make learning lots of fun.

Suggested Activities

- This is the perfect segue to introduce the concept of outlining to students. It is one method of note-taking that utilizes the Roman numerals, and Geisert's book is such a friendly introduction to them.
- Have the students list as many members of their extended family as they possibly can. Then ask them to write all their relatives' ages, using the Roman numeral system. Or, name as many places as they can where Roman numerals are still being used: Pagination for introductions in books is one for your list.
- If your school or school district has a Latin teacher, invite that educator to come and speak to the class about their field of expertise. He or she could stress the significant reasons for knowing something about a "dead" language.
- Working in small groups, students will create original board games that reinforce the concept of Roman numerals. Reserve an entire afternoon in which the games are introduced and then played by the other groups in the classroom.
- I think that Geisert's book is as much about pigs as it is the Roman numerals! It's equally appropriate for the language arts, as well as being perfect for a math curriculum. Why not have students bring in their favorite children's books that contain pigs as main characters? Geisert himself has crafted several other books with pigs in them. In your classroom, prepare language charts that compare and contrast the various pig characters from

the books suggested by the students. Create a display of the collection in the school library. Accompany the collection with a class big book bibliography that lists title, author, illustrator, and publisher information; include a summary of the book, and an illustration of the pig, too.

- If you are really smitten with Geisert's pigs and others like them, you should celebrate National Pig Day, which takes place on March 1. On that day, begin or culminate a theme study of the pig, which is thought to be the most intelligent of domestic animals.

An American Safari: Adventures of the North American Prairie

Jim Brandenburg. 1995. *An American Safari: Adventures of the North American Prairie.* New York: Walker and Company.
ISBN: 0-8027-8320-1

Synopsis

Jim Brandenburg's talent as a superb nature writer and his gift as a fine wildlife photographer combine to produce one of the most notable science picture books to be published in recent years. The topic—the North American prairie—is a subject dear to Brandenburg's heart. His love for the vast, treeless, grasslands region began as a child growing up in southern Minnesota, and flourishes just as fervently today.

Through passionate text and captivating photographic images, Brandenburg celebrates the beauty of the terrain, plants, and animals that compose the American prairie. He also informs readers of the great destruction and near demise that befell this treasured habitat at the hands of our nineteenth-century ancestors, who transformed it into land for farming and raising cattle.

Brandenburg divides the book into five brief chapters. Largely autobiographical, the first chapter tells stories of his youth, especially that of an epiphanic encounter with a red fox, in which Brandenburg decides to "hunt" the grasslands inhabitants with a new camera instead of his customary traps and gun. The remaining chapters feature a verbal and visual exposition of prairie dogs, rattlesnakes, bison, and elk, as well as numerous varieties of grasses, countless wildflowers, and a preponderance of insects, which contribute "to the brilliance and buzz of the region."

A generous amount of white surrounds all words and pictures and accentuates the handsomely designed picture book. The full-color photographs, which range from small vignettes to page-and-a-half panoramas, liberally dot the text and invite perusal. Reading only the captions divulges riveting and worthwhile information.

One full-page photograph in particular stands out singularly for me. In it, Brandenburg's camera focuses on the dark, shadowy outlines of three prairie dog pups "all lined up like little soldiers alongside their mother" as they practice their warning barks one late afternoon. Strikingly set against a shimmering sea of golden grass illuminated by the setting sun, the four rabbit-size rodents look "like candles on a birthday cake." The image pays laudable—and poignant—tribute to what was once a perfectly balanced ecosystem.

In addition to his role as preeminent expert on the American prairie, Brandenburg is also an ardent environmental activist who champions the preservation of that endangered land. Throughout the entire book, he urges all informed citizens to become more actively involved in an effort to "imitate nature rather than trying to control it." An appendix lists names and addresses of organizations that welcome such involvement.

Suggested Activities

- Invite a local wildlife photographer to come and speak to the students about his or her profession. That person should be prepared to share knowledge about helpful training and schooling, the equipment one needs, strategies for capturing the perfect image, and possible career opportunities. Have the photographer bring along his or her portfolio.
- In the appendix of his book, Brandenburg lists the address of the national headquarters of The Nature Conservancy. Write to it to learn about the local chapters of this organization. Volunteer, as a class, to help their local causes; be prepared to commit your efforts for the entire school year.
- Stage a mock debate that argues the presence of prairie dogs on lands presently used for cattle grazing. One team will represent the ranchers, who maintain that they cannot allow prairie dogs to live on the ranges. The other

team will consist of the conservationists, who insist that it's the cows doing the overgrazing and that prairie dogs actually enrich the soils of the prairies.

• Prepare a class anthology of "Prairie Botany," one that contains information about many species of wildflowers found on the North American prairie. Provide detailed color illustrations that accompany your written findings. A great list to begin with includes wild prairie rose, black-eyed Susan, blazing star, purple coneflower, pasqueflower, and the scarlet globe mallow.

• Make arrangements for a wildlife biologist to come and discuss the plight of the black-footed ferret—North America's rarest mammal—which cannot even live in the wild without the presence of prairie dogs. Prior to the guest speaker's visit, read *Phantom of the Prairie: Year of the Black-footed Ferret* (Sierra Club Books for Children, 1998), by Jonathon London and illustrated by Barbara Bash, to learn exactly how the ferrets depend on the prairie dogs for their existence.

Outside and Inside Bats

Sandra Markle. 1997. *Outside and Inside Bats.* New York: Atheneum. Illustrated with photographs. ISBN: 0-689-81165-9

Synopsis

Creator of the extremely successful Outside and Inside animal picture books, Sandra Markle imparts yet another fascinating science lesson, this time teaching readers much about the only mammals capable of powered flight. Markle's text possesses a conversational quality rarely found in nonfiction works, and with it she quickly establishes an amiable rapport with her audience. The accompanying color photographs are equally accessible, sometimes clarifying and extending the text, sometimes relating adequately new information through the use of captions. Verbal and visual components unite seamlessly to invite even the most unenthusiastic students into the intriguing world of bats.

Markle begins this book with an imperative—one that gently commands readers to examine the particular variety of bat pictured in the photograph, a Sanborn's long-nosed bat. She follows with a question: "Do you ever wonder why bats can fly and you can't?" Such an engaging introduction inevitably impels curious readers to turn the pages to discover the answer to that question and others like it.

As if perched comfortably on her readers' shoulders, Markle leads students through the facile discourse. The cogent presentation of text and photographs highlights several different species of bats, discusses unique anatomical features, and shares knowledge about their diets, navigational ways, and reproductive habits.

Markle's book adeptly interacts and connects with its readers so that they grasp more readily any newfound knowledge. Using an enlarged photo of a bat's skeleton and neck bones, she first directs readers to observe the similarity between their own neck bones and those of the bat's: They each have seven neck bones. She then instructs students to tip their heads back as far as they possibly can, thereby introducing the difference: That bats "have neck bones shaped to rotate as freely as your arm does at the shoulder. This lets a bat that is hanging upside down lift its head to eat or to look around." With words and pictures, Markle flawlessly executes a scientific lesson.

Many readers will delight in poring over those pictures that enlarge the inner anatomical workings of bats. One vivid photograph in particular magnifies a bat's stomach to make it as big as a child's fist, its intestine as thick around as a no. 2 pencil! Such a photo has come to represent a Markle trademark. Rather than titillate, it makes one aspect of the lesson perfectly clear; it accomplishes the task so admirably, too.

Reference-wise, this book is superlative. At book's end, Markle provides the name, mailing address, and telephone number of an organization that offers affordably priced plans for building bat houses. Another page poses six additional questions about certain photographic illustrations; all queries provide purposeful opportunities for readers to interact further with the book, augmenting comprehension. A thorough glossary–index and a pronunciation guide are also included.

Suggested Activities

- Bats do not erect their own nesting roosts; they look for warm, dark places such as caves, barns, abandoned buildings, or dead standing trees in which to build their nests. Because these dwellings are quickly disappearing, there is a real need to provide bats homes. For bat house plans, write to the organization Markle mentions in her book. *Beastly Abodes: Homes for Birds, Bats, Butterflies & Other Backyard Wildlife* (Sterling Publishing Co., 1995), by Bobbe Needham, is another excellent resource that offers—within the pages of the book—detailed plans for building five different bat houses. Look for the book in your local library. Ask lumber yards or home builders to donate materials and hardware. Build some bat houses!

- Have a small group of students conduct research to dispel the following bat myths: Bats carry rabies, bats are attracted to human hair, and bat droppings are harmful to your health. Share your discoveries with the class. Be certain to offer proof of your findings.
- Prepare classroom reports for many of the varieties of bats known today; there are close to eight hundred varieties found throughout the world! Include size, wingspan, diet, reproductive habits, location of habitats, and status of endangerment. Have one student report on the already extinct Cuban yellow bat. Share these orally then display reports, along with colorful illustrations, on a classroom or hallway wall.
- Have students read Theodore Roethke's poem entitled "The Bat." Discuss how the poem's last line makes for something of a surprise ending. Encourage students to provide original illustrations to accompany the poem.

For Further Reading

Goodman, Susan E. 1998. *Stones, Bones, and Petroglyphs: Digging into Southwest Archaeology.* Photographs by Michael J. Doolittle. New York: Atheneum/Simon & Schuster. Ebullient eighth graders from Missouri take a field trip to Colorado's Mesa Verde region and explore the archaeological ruins of the Pueblo Indians. Utilizing a scrapbook format, this comprehensive photo essay enthusiastically features hands-on science.

Lasky, Kathryn. 1997. *The Most Beautiful Roof in the World: Exploring the Rainforest Canopy.* Photographs by Christopher G. Knight. San Diego: Gulliver Green/Harcourt Brace. An esteemed nature writer ventures into Central America to document plant ecologist Meg

Lowman's exploration of the rainforest from a rare, treetop vantage point. Revealing color photographs introduce readers to this ecosystem's exceedingly diverse plant and animal life.

McMillan, Bruce. 1998. *Salmon Summer.* Boston: Houghton Mifflin. McMillan's superlative signature color photographs and accessible text document a day in the life of an Alaska Native boy who spends the summer at his family's fishing camp on Kodiak Island in Alaska's pristine wilderness.

Patent, Dorothy Hinshaw. 1996. *Quetzal: Sacred Bird of the Cloud Forest.* Illustrated by Neil Waldman. New York: Morrow. A unique examination of the quetzal, indigenous to Mexico and Central America, highlighting both the historical importance and pending endangered status of this revered feathered animal.

Pringle, Laurence. 1995. *Fire in the Forest: A Cycle of Growth and Renewal.* Illustrated by Bob Marstall. New York: Atheneum/Simon & Schuster. The preeminent science writer debunks the myth of fire as destroyer, elucidating its beneficial powers to regenerate forest ecosystems. Dramatic two-page spreads in fiery hues of red and orange chronicle the natural cycle.

Seymour, Simon. 1997. *The Brain: Our Nervous System.* New York: Morrow. With clear accessible text and dramatically enlarged color photographs, this overview of the remarkable organ responsible for human thought, touch, movement, and memory will likely fascinate and educate novice and expert science students.

Swineburne, Stephen R. 1998. *In Good Hands: Behind the Scenes at a Center for Orphaned and Injured Birds.* San Francisco: Sierra Club/Little, Brown. A laudable photo essay that depicts adolescent Hannah as she volunteers at the Vermont Raptor Center, guiding readers through the process of rescue, rehabilitation, and eventual release of North American birds of prey.

Wexler, Jerome. 1995. *Everyday Mysteries.* New York: Dutton. An interactive book that offers entertaining, unusual looks at ordinary objects found in everyday life. Thirty-six greatly enlarged color photographs provide curious readers opportunities to peruse, ponder, and predict, as they puzzle out the identity of some familiar subjects presented "in new ways."

Chapter 6 Potpourri

One-of-a-Kind Books

> There are all sorts of picture books. There is a place for them all.
>
> —Charlotte Zolotow,
> *The Horn Book Magazine*

When I first began the selection process of deciding which outstanding titles to include in this project, I read literally hundreds of picture books. The most notable of these almost immediately seemed natural and obvious in their groupings, their sorts perfectly suited to consider and discuss together in a chapter. These kinds of picture books quickly became the contents for the five chapters that precede this one. There were, however, other equally meritorious picture books that defied my attempts to group them thematically with others or even within a particular genre. I was stumped as to where to place these desirable, one-of-a-kind picture books.

During those handful of instances in which I fussed over this, I simply set aside the book in question, wondering if I would have the opportunity to highlight it. I gave it no further thought until near the end of my selection process, when I discovered that the picture books I had initially disregarded created a rather impressive group on their own! So impressive, in fact, are these especially unique picture books, I believe they warrant their own chapter. More importantly, because of their prominent picture book qualities, they deserve a place within your classroom, to be enjoyed by you and your students.

Happenstance actually allowed me to unearth this aspect about my own process of choosing which picture books to use within my own classroom. In my quest to find books that—according to my own narrow limitations that I group them together for themed units of study—I thought must somehow "fit together," I happily stumbled on the notion that one notable picture book alone can stand as sufficient reason to justify sharing it with my students. In the future, as you fashion your own selection process to decide which picture books you'll choose for classroom use, I urge you to allow for the possibility of such serendipitous encounters. Find the time and the place to share that one especial picture book with your students.

In an artistic union of Eastern and Western cultures, the first picture book elegantly incarnates a host of heartfelt emotions. The second takes older readers on a jovial jaunt through winsome words and inimitable illustrations. The third picture book vividly recounts a memorable family occasion—that of a wedding—as experienced by a young Latina. The fourth also features a young American; she acts as storyteller, sharing remarkable and poignant family histories of seven of her female ancestors.

Voices of the Heart

Ed Young. 1997. *Voices of the Heart.* New York: Scholastic.
ISBN: 0-590-50199-2

Synopsis

In his ability to create perfect picture books, Ed Young has few equals. As illustrator of over seventy books, fifteen of which he has written, Young exhibits a consummate understanding of how picture book art and text work in tandem. His uncompromising passion and impeccable graphic design sense are two qualities that inform his impressive body of works. Both of these distinctions have, doubtless, helped him garner one Caldecott Medal and two Caldecott Honor Awards during his eminent career in children's literature.

Young was born and raised in China, and for his college studies he came to the United States, where he resides today. The years he spent in China and his cultural heritage greatly influence the picture books he so meticulously crafts, and *Voices of the Heart*—I believe his most aesthetic and personal undertaking to date—is no exception.

Young's 1990 Boston Globe–Horn Book Award acceptance speech, entitled "Eight Matters of the Heart," serves as inspiration for this volume, which focuses on twenty-six Chinese calligraphy characters that contain the heart symbol and express an astonishing array of human feelings. Some of the emotions Young gives voice to by his choice of sundry heart characters—ideograms, he calls them—include *joy,* "a happy heart"; *resentment,* in which "the heart is bitter"; *wrath,* "an angry heart"; *constancy,* "the heart is faithful"; and *mercy,* "a compassionate heart."

The book itself, an oversized horizontal rectangle, measuring a generous twelve by ten inches, houses similarly grand words and pictures of those emotions. Most fetching are Young's highly original visual interpretations of the feelings; they consist of handmade collages that celebrate his personal ties to both the Eastern and Western worlds. They are bold and breathtaking.

For example, Young places the English word *Realization* in the top-left corner of the page, in big, red typeface. Below that, he briefly describes the emotion, "[When:] the heart reaches complete understanding." What then follows is a short explanation of the individual elements that comprise the Chinese ideogram. One element, that of five, signifies senses, elements, colors, and tastes. And, when the heart harmonizes with all of these, it "leads to realization." Young then situates the red Chinese calligraphy symbol in the bottom-left corner, which nicely counterbalances the standard English characters at top.

Finally, to the right of this text, Young fashions a stunning cut-paper collage illustration of the Chinese symbol, adorned by a gently curved, slender pink heart set against a marbleized background in lavender, pale blue, and celadon. Atop the heart rests the Arabic numeral 5, Young's contemporary rendition of the Chinese calligraphy symbol. His artwork depicts in concrete, Western symbols, the more abstract, Eastern calligraphy symbols; in doing so, Young bridges together these two cultures for his audience to appreciate and reflect.

In an author's note, Young reflects on his purpose in making the volume. He writes, "My main intention was to satisfy my curiosity and reach another level of understanding." After taking in this picture book's wisdom and beauty, older readers are certain to come away with their own enhanced understandings of these powerful emotions of the heart.

Suggested Activities

- A shared reading of the book would provide even high school students ample food for thought for lively small-group discussions. The book also makes an excellent introduction to a study of the East and West, in which students examine similarities as well as differences between the two worlds. Young studies and teaches Tai Chi Chuan, which is a regimen of meditation and physical exercise that stems from Chinese cosmology. It would prove fascinating to arrange for someone versed in Tai Chi Chuan to appear before the class as a guest speaker.
- Have the students create their own Chinese accordion books and create their own cut-paper collage interpretations of some of their favorite emotions presented in Young's book. For this activity I have used Susan Kapuscinski Gaylord's *Multicultural Books to Make and Share* (Scholastic Professional Books, 1994), and found that it is an excellent resource for this project and others, too. Gaylord's text lists materials needed and contains thorough, easy-to-follow directions. The finished product is lovely—and makes an ideal gift for parents on special occasions.
- Be as creative as Ed Young: Have students make their own papers to use for their collages in their accordion books. Or, if you like, invite someone versed in Chinese calligraphy to come to your class to instruct your students in that fine art. Complete the accordion books with beautiful Chinese calligraphy.
- Use *Voices of the Heart* to begin an in-depth author study of Ed Young. His voluminous body of published works and the wide range of media he uses to illustrate books will offer students endless opportunities to learn about the making of picture books, as well as provide them with yet another meaningful way to connect with children's literature and one of its master creators. Take this study one step further: Invite Ed Young to make an appearance at your school. This kind of event requires months of advance

planning, a sum of money for an honorarium fee, and the purchase of Young's books for the students to read and respond to prior to the visit; it can, however, be extraordinarily rewarding for teacher and students alike.

Watch William Walk

Ann Jonas. 1997. *Watch William Walk*. New York: Greenwillow.
ISBN: 0-688-14172-2

Synopsis

Utilizing playful alliteration and unusual perspective, Ann Jonas treats older readers to a sheer verbal and visual delight in her most recent, utterly innovative picture book. The jacket cover copy explains Jonas' inspiration for *Watch William Walk*: In her attempt to take alliteration as far as she could, Jonas wrote an entire tale where every word of the text starts with the twenty-third letter of the alphabet! Wow!

And some feat it is. This is not just a pointless, inane tongue-twister exercise in creative writing; it is far from that. Jonas writes convincingly, albeit concisely, of a stroll taken by a boy named William, a dog known as Wally, a girl called Wilma, and a duck named Wanda. The tale begins with the imperative: "Watch William walk with Wally." Turn the page to continue reading that "Wally welcomes William's walks." Never actually sounding forced or contrived, the complete story has a distinct beginning, middle, and end. Furthermore, it contains a cast of major as well as minor characters; it even has a definite plot, conflict, and satisfactory resolution.

With her carefully selected words, Jonas provides a minimal storyline of her tale, essentially about two kids and their pets. With her handsomely crafted illustrations, however, she divulges a maximum amount of information, revealing much about William, Wally, Wilma, and, of course, Wanda—all out and about on a carefree hike one gloriously sunlit day.

Formerly a graphic artist, Jonas illustrates the book by using bold, bright watercolor paints and a black pen. While the full-color artwork is crisp, clean, and indeed, smartly designed, it's the unique aerial perspective

Jonas employs that warrants discussion. Throughout the entire book, readers view only the tops of the human characters' heads, and the tops and backs of the animals. Every two-page spread, in fact, offers readers a bird's-eye view of all scenes depicted.

In her pictures, Jonas ingeniously includes human footprints and animal tracks, as well as the telling shadows of William, Wilma, Wally, and Wanda. Painted in a soft, muted shade of gray, these two visual components add significantly to the illustrations' narrative strength. Through footprints and tracks—nowhere mentioned in the text—observers see that Wilma walks barefoot and that Wally the dog has a penchant for making crazy eight figures as he patiently waits for his master, William, to catch up to him. And through the four characters' silhouettes, viewers connect the more complicated top-view images with the more familiar side-view figures, even though they appear upside-down, just as a shadow would.

As usual, Jonas' text placement frolics all over the pages and adds considerably to overall narrative content. The large, black typeface captures the insouciant mood of the merry amblers, at times paralleling the gentle contours of the water's edge or following Wanda's wake when the duck swims in the wetlands. With this creative picture book, Jonas crafts story and illustrations in fresh, new ways; she takes readers on untrodden pathways that lead to imaginative fun with words and pictures.

Suggested Activities

- This is an opportune time to introduce, reinforce, or simply have some fun with the literary device known as alliteration. Have students write their own alliterative texts, attempting to craft stories with believable characters and a likely plot. Suggest that students also illustrate their texts, perhaps with the same bird's-eye perspective Jonas employs in her picture book.
- Take a serious look at alliteration. Search for instances of it in various volumes of poetry and prose. Obtain a copy of Shakespeare's *A Midsummer Night's Dream*; discover what kind of fun the world-famous playwright had with alliteration. Display examples of alliteration on a classroom bulletin board.
- Have your students create an alphabet Big Book full of original alliterative phrases from A–Z. For inspiration, read Anita Lobel's dazzling

Alison's Zinnia (Greenwillow, 1990). Accompany the class-crafted text with colorful illustrations. Share the publication with a second- or third-grade class that might just be learning about alliteration and donate the creation to their classroom library.

- Invite the art teacher from your own school—or one from your school district—to come for a lecture–slide presentation on perspectives in art. Ask that instructor to define and discuss such terms as *parallel, angular,* and *oblique perspectives*. Introduce other more familiar terms that include *bird's-eye view, worm's-eye view,* and *eye-level view*. Provide ample opportunity to look closely at examples of all three perspectives. Have students engage in drawing pictures that demonstrate the various perspectives and then articulate the meanings that each connotes.
- Have students write some original alliterative tongue-twisters. Hold a class contest to determine who can repeat the greatest number of tongue-twisters with the fewest number of errors. Award the winner a pocket-sized paperback thesaurus or dictionary of literary terms.

Snapshots from the Wedding

Gary Soto. 1997. *Snapshots from the Wedding*. New York: Putnam.
ISBN: 0-399-22808-X

Synopsis

Author Gary Soto's delicious words find such able companionship in Stephanie Garcia's charming three-dimensionally constructed illustrations that, together, they form a harmonious union that makes this picture book one to remember. When reading this treasure, it's as if Maya, the flower girl who recalls the happy wedding celebrated by her Mexican American family, has snuggled cozily beside you on your living room sofa, eager to recount the joyous occasion. Family "album" in hand, you do relive the felicity and excitement of the very special day when Isabel and Rafael marry, as experienced through the immediacy of Maya's naive, though keen, senses.

She begins her first-person narrative with what's obviously most important to her: "Here's me, Maya, / Flower girl with flowers in my hair." Her acumen for observing even the tiniest details informs us that ring bearer Danny's left shoe is untied, and that the altar boy assisting Father Jaime suffers from ennui—note the illustration in which he's yawning—and wears a dirty sneaker, too.

Maya's words sound genuinely childlike, but poetic, as when she describes the lovely bride, Isabel: "Her hands soft as doves." Maya also discerns another special feature about the ceremony and Isabel: "The candles sparkle, almost heart-shaped with flame" / And almost as bright as her eyes." As heavenly as the bride looks, Rafael the groom appears far less ethereal: He sports a casted arm, from a recent softball injury. Maya retorts, "I think it makes him look brave *y guapo*," which a welcome introductory glossary defines as "good looking." Maya fluently sprinkles such Spanish words throughout her entire narration, which adds veracity to the conversational tone the text possesses.

The ceremony concludes with cheers and tears; then it's off to the reception, but not before Maya's tuxedo-clad uncle, Tío Trino—readers glimpse him with a hankie to his forehead, carefully avoiding any grease and grime—jump-starts someone's car. At the festivities, Maya reports that family members enjoy partaking in a bowl of ripe olives and authentic Mexican dishes of *pollo con mole, arroz y frijoles*; listening to mariachis' music; feasting on a wedding cake "With more frosting than a mountain of snow, / With more roses than *mi abuela's* back yard."

Like any photograph album, in which a picture's worth a thousand words, Garcia's laudable illustrations deserve praise. She places both art and text against a pale pink and pretty white lace background that mirrors the fabric of Maya's flower girl frock. It makes the book's design as comely as Maya herself and strengthens the union of art and text.

Created from Sculpy clay, wood, fabric, and an array of found objects, the three-dimensional scenes appear as dioramas, often with one particular character highlighted within a gold, wooden frame—hence, the unselfconscious snapshot effect of the illustrations. For one, Maya bedecks her five fingers with ripe olives; a second depicts a partial view of Maya's feet, sans shoes, perched on her daddy's wing tips, dancing together. Framed off for viewers to admire, these vividly distinct images also allow readers to recognize that families, regardless of cultural origins, often commemorate universal experiences that make them far more similar than different.

Suggested Activities

• Have students make lists of those unforgettable experiences that are still personally meaningful and very significant to them. Some of these vivid events might include important "firsts": the very first day of kindergarten; the first time you drove alone; the first day of your first part-time job; the first time you ever flew all by yourself; the first time you went to camp; the first time you overnighted at a friend's house; your first day of high school.

• Another list might describe the funnest time of your life: when your family went on vacation, a rafting or camping trip, to Yellowstone Park; when your eighth-grade American History class went to Washington, D.C., for one week during spring break; when your French class went to Paris for ten days; when your grandparents took you to Disney World during winter break. Still other topics for important events include your sixteenth birthday; the day your older sibling went off to college; a special wedding within your extended family; your eighth-grade graduation ceremony; the day you finally got your very own horse.

• On a sadder note, you might ask for tragic or traumatic events: the day a hurricane or flood devastated your community; the loss of a best friend; the death of a grandparent; when your family moved to another state; when you wrecked your parents' car. And, on a lighter note, ask students to write about one of the most embarrassing or funniest days of their lives: kissing a boyfriend and both sets of braces lock together; wearing two different colored socks to school; some hilarious family anecdote from early childhood.

• Have each student select one of these memorable times to write about. They should use first-person voice in their narratives. They should try to recall the experience or occasion with as much accuracy and emotion as possible. They might want to record first the literal events, and then fill in with sensorial detail. Have them think about it from the perspective of all five senses and then incorporate that into their writing, as Maya does so capably.

They should choose their words carefully, providing as much detail as possible. Have them share with a classmate for peer editing. They should type their final draft and mount it on colorful mat board.

- Using the same media, such as Sculpy clay, found objects, wood, fabric, and acrylic paints, fashion dioramas similar to the ones in *Snapshots from the Wedding*. Each student's scene should represent one of the more poignant images from the experience about which they have written. Spend an entire afternoon, sharing with your class the finished writing assignments and art projects. Display them proudly in the classroom when parents come for an open house or back-to-school evening; this project would be perfect for such an event.

Seven Brave Women

Betsy Hearne. 1997. *Seven Brave Women.* New York: Greenwillow.
ISBN: 0-688-14502-7

Synopsis

In this estimable picture book, an adolescent narrator sets the stage with a quietly dramatic introduction that begins, "In the old days, history books marked time by the wars that men fought." Men and wars, however, have little to do with the subject matter of this lovely volume. As the title suggests, these remembrances—eight very brief chapters that more closely resemble vignettes—exalt the "unsung heroes," the female ancestors whose endless hard work, sheer determination, and true grit helped to shape this family's notable lineage.

The narrator pays fitting tribute to the intrepid women in her family "who made history by not fighting in wars," as she chronicles her heartfelt family stories with a time line of all the wars the United States has waged. Anaphora marks all the chapters' openings—and imbues the narrator's voice with a superb storytelling quality—with a phrase very similar to the first: "My great-great-great-grandmother did great things. Elizabeth lived during the Revolutionary War, but she did not fight in it." A devout Mennonite, the young Swiss bravely crossed the Atlantic in a wooden ship with two babies in tow, pregnant with her third, and settled in Pennsylvania, only to have her ninth child at the age of fifty.

In the fifth vignette, the narrator recounts: "My grandmother did great things. Betty lived during World War II, but she did not fight in it." She went to school to become an architect at a time when it was strictly a male profession. Betty designed and built the home that she lived in with her family. To take a walk with Betty, "made you look at walls and windows in a new way." Even in her eighties, she wrote two books about architecture.

Rendered in oil paints on a gesso background, richly textured full-color illustrations capture the heroic strength and resoluteness shared by the featured relatives. Oversized double-page spreads in vividly intense pastel hues depict each of the remarkable females ensconced in equally remarkable activities.

For Betty, the architect, readers glimpse her hard at work erecting the frame of a structure. Hammer in hand, two nails held at the ready between her lips, this grandmother wears bright blue carpenter's overalls and a tool belt around her waist. She studies architectural blueprints with a countenance that displays not only knowledge and expertise about her craft, but also a sense of satisfaction; Betty is happy at what she is doing.

Throughout the entire book, a pair of doves—one appears on the introductory page, the other after an author's note—fly a beak-held magenta ribbon that ties the lives of these women together. Birds and woven strip suggest the peaceful lineage these ancestors comprise and serve as a unifying theme for all eight chapters. Shaped by a testimonial text and inspirational illustrations, genealogy has never been more engagingly presented, especially for a young adult audience.

Suggested Activities

- Put together a class album about some of the students' brave women ancestors; if there are nineteen students, entitle your book *Nineteen Brave Women*. Have each student choose a remarkable female ancestor about whom to write. Pattern the anecdotal essays after Betsy Hearne's chapters, beginning with a similar anaphoral phrase. Example: "My great-great grandmother did great things. Alma May lived during World War I, but she did not fight in it." Photocopy actual photos of all students' relatives as part of the illustrations for the class book. Display them in the school library.

- Working in small groups, students will research particular women who have achieved great things. Possible topics might include Mary McLeod Bethune, Sara Josepha Hale, Helen Beatrix Potter, Annie Smith Peck, Maria Mitchell, Anne Carroll Moore, Lucretia Mott, Pearl S. Buck, or Gwendolyn Brooks. Students will share in the form of oral presentations, as well as create some interesting visual aids for their reports. Create a classroom bulletin board to showcase the small groups' findings.
- Celebrate Grandma Moses Day, an official holiday that commemorates the birthday of Anna Mary Robertson Moses. Known as Grandma Moses, this brave woman began painting when she was seventy-eight years old, and continued her artistic career for nearly twenty-five years more. Ask your school librarian for a video about the life and paintings of Grandma Moses; show it to the class. Invite a locally renowned folk art painter to come and speak to the class about this particular style of art, also called naive art. Students can then create their own naive-style paintings.
- Investigate the life and accomplishments of Mother Teresa, who, in 1979, was awarded the Nobel Peace Prize for her missionary work throughout the world. Have students respond to the following quotation by Mother Teresa: "We can do no great things, only small things with great love." How does this maxim apply to the seven brave women featured in Betsy Hearne's book? Have the students generate a list of those women who have achieved "small things with great love," and then share their findings in the form of oral presentations.
- Have the entire class research the inception and development of the women's rights movement in the United States. Begin with the year 1848, in which the first women's rights convention took place at Seneca Falls, New York. Small groups may want to prepare oral presentations of such luminaries as Elizabeth Cady Stanton, Lucretia Mott, and Susan B. Anthony. Focus on the contributions these women made to feminism as we know it today.
- Make a time line of important dates and events that document the history of the women's movement. Start with 1848 and continue to the present day; be sure to highlight well-known contemporary leaders, which include Eleanor Roosevelt, Gertrude Stein, and Gloria Steinem.

For Further Reading

Cisneros, Sandra. 1994. *Hairs = Pelitos*. Illustrated by Terry Ybáñez. New York: Knopf. This is an excerpt from one of the author's books for adults that celebrates the many different kinds of hair a young girl describes her Hispanic family as having. Primitive-style paintings in a uniquely expressionistic palette accompany the English and Spanish texts.

Coy, John. 1996. *Night Driving*. Illustrated by Peter McCarty. New York: Holt. Black-and-white pencil drawings in gently rounded shapes evoke the 1950s, as they depict the all-night road trip taken by a loving father and his excited son across the plains to their destination in the mountains.

Macaulay, David. 1997. *Rome Antics*. Boston: Houghton Mifflin. A homing pigeon proves to be an intrepid as well as unusual guide when it takes readers on a whirling tour of Rome and its architectural landmarks, rendered for readers in Macaulay's inimitable pen-and-ink line drawings.

Martin, Jacqueline Briggs. 1996. *Grandmother Bryant's Pocket*. Pictures by Petra Mathers. Boston: Houghton Mifflin. Traumatized by a barn fire that kills her dog, eight-year-old Sarah spends time with her herbalist grandmother and cooper grandfather so that she may heal. The simple text and numerous vignettes delicately depict late eighteenth-century rural Maine.

Raschka, Chris. 1997. *Mysterious Thelonious*. New York: Orchard. A hand-lettered text and bold watercolors innovatively pair the musical chromatic scale with the hues of the color wheel to pay unique homage to Thelonius Monk, the great African American jazz composer and his renowned work, "Misterioso."

Sisulu, Elinor Batezat. 1996. *The Day Gogo Went to Vote: South Africa, April 1994*. Illustrated by Sharon Wilson. Boston: Little, Brown. Richly textured pastels reflect the multilayered significance of South Africa's first democratic elections, as they detail a young girl's trip accompanying her great-grandmother, a first-time voter, to the polling booth.

Stewart, Sarah. 1997. *The Gardener.* Pictures by David Small. New York: Farrar, Straus, & Giroux. Depression doldrums uproot young Lydia Grace from her parents' farm, temporarily transporting her to Uncle Jim's urban bakery and its upstairs apartment. The epistolary text and homey line drawings lovingly record the flowering of family relationships and the promise of better times.

Tunnell, Michael O. 1997. *Mailing May.* Illustrated by Ted Rand. New York: Tambourine/Greenwillow. Because her folks cannot afford the fare, five-year-old Charlotte May gets "mailed" to a grandmother who lives miles away, journeying as baggage aboard a train's mail car. Based on an actual incident, the book's telling watercolors include details reminiscent of early twentieth-century life in the U.S. Northwest.

Conclusion

Choosing Picture Books for Classroom Use

> The conclusion is simple. Picture books can do just about everything other kinds of books can do, and in the vibrations between words and pictures, sometimes more.
>
> —Barbara Bader,
> *The Horn Book Magazine*

Barbara Bader's words resound with astonishing clarity and veracity when I consider the educational results that picture books have offered me and my students. In my discussion of the outstanding books highlighted within these pages, I have attempted to demonstrate the vast learning potential that words and pictures together portend for older readers. Like Comenius, I have come to believe that learning is enhanced when presented verbally and visually. I know firsthand the knowledge and the pleasure my students and I have profited from while engaging in various activities related to the noteworthy picture books we have read together. Sharing these picture books and others like them has been enormously rewarding for my students, not to mention the gains I believe it brings me in my quest to know more about children's literature.

The picture books I showcase represent only a handful of titles that deserve places among the shelves in your own classroom collection or in your all-school library. Even the additional lists of superb picture books that appear at each chapter's end suggest just a few other notable selections. Altogether, this book features seventy-six titles—not many, compared with the thousands of picture books still in print today or to the hundreds of new titles that are published annually. Quite logically, then, I ask myself the following: What about the myriad picture books besides the ones I've chosen to discuss here? Are these seventy-six the only titles to use with older readers? Absolutely not, and here are the reasons why.

First, much of the in-depth discourse about the various titles I examined simply honed my own evaluative process of how best to select from among the plethora of existing and newly published picture books. In my attempt to articulate what any one of the seventy-six picture books' verbal and visual strengths was, I improved my own skill of looking critically at all picture books.

Second, I queried, "Why is that so important to me?" Well, I am certain that throughout this endeavor I have gained a greater appreciation of this genre of children's literature. I also know that when I do choose picture books from among the thousands of titles still in print and the hundreds of new releases every year, my decision now will be an even more informed one than before this undertaking.

Third, I'm absolutely certain that as I increased my own understanding of why some picture books were highly successful, the pleasure I derived from using the best picture books in my own classroom increased concomitantly. It is truly exciting for me to think about all the picture books I have yet to read which hold the promise of enhancing learning for older readers. They include those picture books that perhaps have become forgotten gems, or even those that their gifted creators have yet to craft. All of these picture books, because of their resonance between text and illustration, can generate the same kind of exciting learning that other classroom books can, and as critic Barbara Bader suggests, "sometimes more."

Finally, I want to leave you with a close look at two specific picture books—both of which ably demonstrate the selection process I implement in choosing titles—and how they figure significantly, but radically differently, into my own classroom teaching experience. The two titles represent the extreme ends of what I'll call the picture book spectrum; they also emphasize the importance of simply reading and really thinking about picture books when considering them for use with older readers.

At one end of this continuum lies the picture book that first provided the tiny seed for this project to flourish into a book: *Tomorrow's Alphabet,* by George Shannon, with pictures by Donald Crews (Greenwillow, 1996). It is in the realm reserved for books that others deem as appropriate only for the very youngest readers. By all initial appearances, *Tomorrow's Alphabet* seems ideally suited for teaching a youngster the ABCs and their sounds. One could quickly dismiss it as obviously far too simple for any older readers to respond to, let alone learn from.

Then, at the other end of the continuum lies the second picture book, one I have yet to use in my classroom: *Harlem,* by Walter Dean Myers, with pictures by Christopher Myers (Scholastic, 1997). This title is very sophisticated and "grown-up" in its content, design, and format. It might well be deemed a picture book for adults—if there were such an entity—and certainly appropriate for young adults' appreciation.

When I first read *Tomorrow's Alphabet,* I was quite intrigued with the passage of time in this slim, handsome volume. Author George Shannon, in the briefest text imaginable, creates for readers an intellectually challenging game that is both sophisticated and demanding. He gives each letter a two-page spread: For example, on the left-hand page, participants read "A is for seed—." On the opposite page: "tomorrow's APPLE" provides the answer and the reason a seed could ever represent the letter A—because with time, it grows into an apple.

Donald Crews' illustrations, realistic watercolors placed against a generously white background, introduce big, concrete images. In the top left-hand corner stands a grass-green capital A, three inches tall and just as wide. Below the minimal text one sees an oversized hand with a tiny brown seed resting in an open palm. A second outstretched hand appears on the opposite page: a ripe, red apple that's even larger than the A rests in this palm. Just above the hand, the word *tomorrow's,* and just below the hand, one reads the word *APPLE,* in inch-high letters colored the same grass-green. Immediately, one sees the connection: A is for *apple,* which started out as a seed. Words and pictures provide twenty-five other puzzles for readers to ponder over.

Meanwhile, back at school, my students and I were very near the culmination of a terrific themed study of the Middle Ages. It occurred to me one day that *Tomorrow's Alphabet* could figure significantly into the conclusion of this unit of study. Here's how: After reading *Tomorrow's Alphabet* as a read-aloud to the class, we started to brainstorm the possibilities of creating our own book using the same format. A is for steel—tomorrow's ARMOR; E is for sword—tomorrow's EXCALIBUR; or, K is for page—tomorrow's KNIGHT; H is for Bilbo Baggins—tomorrow's HERO, and so on.

I think my students also improved on the format some. Instead of placing the same letter on both pages of a two-page spread, they suggested putting the puzzle part—the first half of the letter information—on the right-hand page of their picture book, so that participants could supply guesses first, and then turn the page to find the answer on the left-hand side of the following two-page spread.

Furthermore, instead of ordinary uppercase letters, the students drew exquisitely detailed illuminations, the kinds of letters that, indeed, adorned manuscripts from medieval times. The resulting book was a glorious work of art as well as a perfect vehicle to express their understanding of the knowledge gained from their studies.

As the book's flap copy also suggests, what about creating *Yesterday's Alphabet*? B is for muffin—yesterday's BANANA; or, C is for pickle—yesterday's CUCUMBER, and so on. And I began to wonder: What about using *Tomorrow's Alphabet* in other curricular areas? Say Earth Science or American History? Little did I know that I might use this simple, unassuming picture book as a construct with which to look at other subjects in my classroom. For *Tomorrow's Alphabet*, the possibilities are extant; they need only to be tapped.

Now, back to *Harlem*. When I first read it, I was, quite literally, awestruck. Such energy, substance, and true sense of time and place, all housed in a picture book format. Walter Dean Myers, who is—he grew up in New York City's Harlem—one of today's leading voices in African American literature for children and young adults, writes the text. Myers' son, Christopher, with his dramatically kinetic collage art, marks his debut as picture book illustrator.

Poem and pictures combine to revel in a celebration of Harlem: as a neighborhood, a community, and a particular place in which Americans practiced urban living. Verbal and visual components celebrate the music, art, and literature of the cultural capital of Black America. *Harlem* is unlike any other picture book I have ever read.

Growing up in the rural Midwest geographically displaces me from Harlem; to my displeasure today, I realize I know very little about this unique and special locale. But when I read, "A new sound, raucous and sassy / Cascading over the asphalt village / Breaking against the black sky over / 1-2-5 Street. / Announcing hallelujah / Riffing past resolution"; and when I see the accompanying intense illustration of an African American woman, clad in vibrant orange, white-turbaned, her arms reaching out to connect with the energy of the "Place, sound, / Celebration," known as Harlem, I immediately make the commitment to roll up my sleeves to learn what I need to know about Harlem.

What exactly does that mean? Well, I've just returned from my local public library, with four books in hand. Nikki Giovanni's *Shimmy Shimmy Shimmy Like My Sister Kate: Looking at the Harlem Renaissance through Poems* (Henry Holt, 1996) will likely serve as a resource book, providing me with the necessary background information. For starters, reading its introduction alone offers a storehouse of knowledge. Newbery Honor Book *Scorpions* (Harper, 1988), also by Walter Dean Myers, makes for probable read-aloud matter, with Harlem as that story's setting; I read it years ago, but will reread it with renewed purpose. The last two are picture books created by Faith Ringgold. Coincidentally, she was born in Harlem in 1930, and her *Tar Beach* (Crown, 1991) and *Dinner at Aunt Connie's House* (Hyperion, 1993) are two titles I will look at closely in my effort to share *Harlem* with my students in an informed and masterful manner. I am enthused to learn what lies between these picture books' covers.

As I look and learn myself, I remain equally excited about the prospect of sharing *Harlem* with older readers, and also other titles I have yet to discover. With their brief texts and narrative illustrations, picture books are precisely the kind of verbal and visual entities that will not only enlarge older readers' understanding of their world, but also—just as Comenius asserted—give much pleasure in doing so. With picture books, readers have the opportunity to look—and learn.

Bibliography of Picture Book Reference Works

Alderson, Brian. 1973. *Looking at Picture Books, 1973.* Catalog for an exhibition by the National Book League. Oxford, England.

Bader, Barbara. 1976. *American Picturebooks: From Noah's Ark to the Beast Within.* New York: Macmillan.

Bang, Molly. 1991. *Picture This: Perception and Composition.* Boston: Little, Brown.

Brown, Marcia. 1986. *Lotus Seeds: Children, Pictures and Books.* New York: Scribner.

Cummings, Pat, comp. and ed. 1992. *Talking with Artists.* 2 vols. New York: Bradbury.

Egoff, Sheila. 1980. *Only Connect: Readings on Children's Literature, 2d. Ed.* New York: Oxford University Press.

Hearne, Betsy and Marilyn Kaye, eds. 1981. *Celebrating Children's Books: Essays on Children's Literature in Honor of Zena Sutherland.* New York: Lothrop.

Hearne, Betsy, ed. 1993. *The Zena Sutherland Lectures: 1983–1992.* New York: Clarion.

Hearne, Betsy and Roger Sutton, eds. 1993. *Evaluating Children's Books: A Critical Look.* Urbana-Champaign, IL: University of Illinois.

Lacy, Lyn Ellen. 1986. *Art and Design in Children's Picture Books.* Chicago: American Library Association.

Lurie, Alison. 1990. *Don't Tell the Grown-ups: Subversive Children's Literature.* Boston: Little, Brown.

Marantz, Kenneth and Sylvia. 1988. *The Art of Children's Picture Books: A Selective Reference Guide.* New York: Garland.

Marcus, Leonard S. 1988. *A Caldecott Celebration: Six Artists and Their Paths to the Caldecott Medal.* New York: Walker.

Nodelman, Perry. 1988. *Words About Pictures: The Narrative Art of Children's Picture Books.* Athens, GA: University of Georgia Press.

Sendak, Maurice. 1988. *Caldecott and Co.: Notes on Books and Pictures.* New York: Farrar, Straus, & Giroux.

Silvey, Anita, ed. 1995. *Children's Books and Their Creators.* Boston: Houghton Mifflin.

Schulevitz, Uri. 1985. *Writing with Pictures: How to Write and Illustrate Children's Books.* New York: Watson-Guptill.

Townsend, John Rowe. 1990. *Written for Children: An Outline of English Children's Literature, 4th Ed.* New York: HarperCollins.